INDIAN WRITERS
ON
WRITING

INDIAN WRITERS ON WRITING

D. Ramakrishna

Prestige

an international publishing house

Published by

Prestige Books

3/28, East Patel Nagar

New Delhi 110 008

Ph. 9818755529

email: prestigebooks@gmail.com

website: asiabookclub.com

ISBN: 81-7551-195-8

Published 2007

Printed at Chaman Offset Press, New Delhi 110 002

Contents

Preface
7

Literary Criticism

Contemporary Indian English Literary Scene
9

Letters

Mulk Raj Anand
26

Nissim Ezekiel
93

Nayantara Sahgal
120

Seshendra Sarma
125

for

Srinivasa

Preface

In the course of my research on Indian English Writing and Comparative Literature since the mid-1970s, I have extensively corresponded with Mulk Raj Anand, Nissim Ezekiel, Nayantara Sahgal and Seshendra Sarma. Provoked by my questionnaires and letters, they wrote scores of letters to me expressing their views on art and life. Their reactions reflect on the *oeuvre* of each of them, revealing new facets of their writings dealing with Indian culture, traditional and modern.

In his letter of January 21, 1977, Mulk Raj Anand deals with the emergent novel form in India in the context of fragmented cultures, referring to his lectures on the origins and growth of the Indian novel at Panjab University. He writes about "the breakdown of everything in our age, and more than the breakdown the dispersal of cultures." He says in his letter of August 11, 1977: "In fact, I feel that unless my attitude to the experience of creative works in other media and words is understood, there will be always complete misconception about my labyrinthine situations where the self is making itself by breaking itself and remaking itself again and again." The overall picture of Anand that emerges from his letters is that of a great exponent of Indian Culture and Art.

Nissim Ezekiel, a major Indian English poet, editor and essayist, was deeply concerned with life and Art, as evident in his letters like the one of May 12, 1984. As editor of *The Indian P.E.N.*, Ezekiel's involvement with the multiple aspects of Indian culture and literature and as Editor of *Freedom First*, his involvement with the contemporary social and political issues is indisputable. In his letters to me he comments on these facets of his literary activity.

Nayantara Sahgal, the distinguished Indian English novelist, deals with the urban life involving politicians and bureaucrats. She emphasizes the conflict between tradition and modernity in India today, as in her answers to my questionnaire and her letter of August 5, 1978.

Modern Indian literature in English translation is gaining currency in the university departments, having been included in M.A. (English) courses. The works of the leading modern Telugu poet and critic, Seshendra Sarma, are prescribed for study in such courses. The Central Sahitya Akademi Award-winning poet has been translated into English, French, German, and Greek besides several Indian languages including Hindi, Urdu, Bengali and Kannada. He has also written extensively in English on both the traditional and modern Indian culture. In addition to discussing multiple aspects of Indian culture in his letters to me, he has analyzed Jessie Weston's *From Ritual to Romance* (used by T.S. Eliot in writing *The Waste Land*) about Indian mythology and folklore.

The article titled "Contemporary Indian English Literary Scene," prefixed to the letters, deals with Indian English Writing (largely poetry and fiction) past and present in the context of multiplicity and fragmentation of Indian culture to show continuities and divergences.

D. RAMAKRISHNA

Contemporary Indian English Literary Scene

Contemporary Indian English Writing has indeed grown into a significant aspect of world literature. One can notice in this writing a development parallel to the multifaceted advancement of the Indian society since Independence. What was largely a nationalistic writing during the times of Rabindranath Tagore and Sri Aurobindo has become a literature of immense aesthetic and socio-cultural significance for modern India.

According to Adil Jussawalla, Indian writing in English today "reflects the Indian petty bourgeoisie's present inability to find a dynamic role for itself in a society which is slowly transforming itself from the semi-feudal to the capitalist. Wedged between the class that employs it and the broad masses of peasants and the growing urban proletariat, it can only torment itself with its own contradictions or turn on itself in a fury of self-destruction. This is the writing of a bourgeoisie at a dead end."[1] Jussawalla thus sees the individual and the social contradictions embodied in the contemporary Indian writing. In fact, this writing reflects the complex state of the modern Indian society balancing itself between the capitalist and the proletariat extremes. And the Indian writers in English have generally been successful in fusing the socio-cultural values with the aesthetic, keeping pace with the intellectual currents in the outside world. With a superb mastery over the English language, these writers have evolved a distinct idiom suited to the Indian sensibility. Their language and mode of expression are no longer derivative and writing for them has become the most serious literary vocation.

I

Poets like Nissim Ezekiel. A.K. Ramanujan, Kamala Das, R. Parthasarathy, Shiv K. Kumar, Pritish Nandy and Jayanta Mahapatra have won recognition both in India and abroad. They have improved much upon the writing of their predecessors, while consciously or unconsciously repeating certain themes and motifs common to the earlier writing. During the Sixties, Indian poetry in English recorded a distinct departure and the Seventies have shown another step in the enormous growth of the writing. Thus Ezekiel's collection of 1965, Kamala Das's *Summer in Calcutta*, A.K. Ramanujan's *The Striders*, Shiv K. Kumar's *Cobwebs in the Sun*, and R. Parthsarathy's *Rough Passage* have given a new direction to the writing of poetry in English.

According to Parthasarathy, "Poems like 'Night of the Scorpion' and 'A River' by their visions of an everyday Indian reality expressed in an unobtrusive personal voice stood out in the reader's mind as signposts indicating the directions poetry in English was likely to take in the future."[2] The kind of "Indian reality" that Parthasarathy finds in the contemporary Indian poetry in English is somewhat limited: it is a consciousness largely shaped by the urban life style of the elite confined to the drawing rooms. Ezekiel's attempt at evoking the rural milieu in "Night of the Scorpion" is that of a city-dweller. While he gives expression to a very personal kind of religion, his stance is that of an ironist too. Even the major poets like Ezekiel have not entirely caught the colour of life of the millions living outside the cities. To them the average or sub-standard Indian is the dweller of the city slums. How about the rural folks who constitute the bulk of the Indian population? Also, in the words of the novelist Mulk Raj Anand, "Apart from the task of seeing human relations, the permanent task of liberating the human soul in travail, the compassion necessary before affliction and pain, and the courageous conferment of one's own freedom on others, remain genuine ideals before the creative intelligentsia."[3]

Such humanistic utterances are dubbed "leftist" by the self-conscious and foppish "creative intelligentsia" to whom Anand is vainly appealing. The writings of great English poets like P.B. Shelley, Alfred Tennyson and Matthew Arnold served as clarion calls to their contemporaries toward a new social and cultural awareness. The poetry of Rabindranath Tagore and Sri Aurobindo achieved this goal in the India of their times, carrying across the continents messages of good-will for international amity. The Indian poets writing in English today seem to be too circumscribed in their vision to present the wider "Indian reality" to the world community.

In a majority of these poets is conspicuously absent a sense of the Indian myth that brings the novels of Raja Rao and R.K. Narayan so close to the hearts of the Indian readers. In the writings of Tagore and Sri Aurobindo too, there is discernible a distinct awareness of such an Indian myth. But the contemporary poets do not generally accept the "Indianness" of the reality presented in these older poets. Thus Adil Jussawalla says: "To my mind . . . *Savitri*, a poem on the relation of the spirit to matter, unwinding like an interminable sari through twelve books and about 2400 lines is one vast onion of a poem. The layers gradually fall away to reveal nothing."[4] Jussawalla questions a tradition which, in his view, is nothing but "a vagueness of thought, an absolute faith in the mystical, and a blind reliance in the heart." He thus fails to see the possible symbolic relevance of the mythological Savitri to the Indian womanhood. Sir Philip Sidney who in *An Apology for Poetry* maintains that the poet is superior to the philosopher, concedes that even "the philosophers of Greece durst not a long time appear to the world but under the masks of poets." Like those great philosophers of Greece, Indian poet-philosophers like Tagore and Sri Aurobindo might be conveying an idealistic view of life through poetry. The question is whether philosophy can be the subject of modern poetry.

Kamala Das's verse is often compared with the confessional poetry of Anne Sexton and Sylvia Plath. On a close reading, however, one gains the impression that her poetry is not entirely an "autobiography of a fever" of the Plath type. Sex in her poetry is often overplayed to the point of nausea and to the detriment of the finer hues of the salubrious familial love. Nevertheless, there seems to be a certain amount of sincerity in an occasional poem like "An Introduction." Parthasarathy, with his relatively limited bulk of writing, has established himself as one of the important poets whose style is marked by exquisite polish. Poems in *Rough*

Passage reveal him as a poet of "self" in search of identity. He is generally lost in a linguistic paradox and turns to Tamil as his language of communication. Jayanta Mahapatra has written some brilliant verse. He is more authentic in the poems on Orissa than in those dealing with love, marriage, and parenthood. He occasionally deals with topical subjects in poems like "Gandhi," "The Tattooed Taste" and "The Twenty-Fifth Anniversary of a Republic."

Parthasarathy's problem with language as a vehicle of poetic utterance is but a part of the larger cultural dilemma that the Indian poet in English is confronted with. In the words of A.K. Ramanujan, "English and my disciplines [linguistics, anthropology] give me my 'outer' forms—linguistic, metrical, logical and other such ways of shaping experience; and my first thirty years in India, my frequent visits and field trips, my personal and professional preoccupations with Kannada, Tamil, the Classics and folklore give me my substance, my 'inner' forms, images and symbols. They are continuous with each other, and I no longer can tell what comes from where."[5]

In Ramanujan's poems like "Conventions of Despair" and "Prayer to Lord Murugan" a tension between "tradition" and "individual talent" is evident. And the poet at times seems to be unable to resolve that tension. This attempt at ordering experience out of the tension between "the brown skin" and Western "bleachers" is a noteworthy feature of Shiv K. Kumar's poetry too.[8] The common charge in respect of Kumar's poetry is that he confuses sex with religion in poems like "Wife at Prayer," "To a Prostitute," and "At a Convent." The sexual fantasies in his poetry (also common to the poetry of Parthasarathy, Kamala Das, and Ezekiel) need not deter one's appreciation of the essential Kumar—the "real Me" of Walt Whitman "with peals of distant ironical laughter"[7] at the contemporary situation. It is his superb handling of irony that gives Kumar a unique place in contemporary Indian poetry in English. Poems like "The Sun Temple of Konarak" make it evident that the sexual imagery in Kumar's poetry is inspired by the erotic motifs on the Sun temple of Konarak—motifs that signify a profound synthesis of the sensual and the spiritual.

While such is the brilliance of a handful of luminaries on the firmament of Indian poetry in English, their lustre is often clouded by the multiplicity of dim figures and shooting stars across the horizon. Perhaps they become more conspicuous on account of the contrasting presence of the lesser figures. The proliferation of these inferior poets has recently been attaining alarming proportions. Almost every second Indian citizen thinks that he is a poet. Particularly in the academic community, it has become a fashion to scribble some lines called "poetry" or at least to publicly exhibit one's enthusiasm for poetry. The craze of the day seems to be that an academic should concoct at least one poem before he retires!

As one enters the world of great poetry, one experiences an orchestral symphony—a symphony of the human spirit. In the words of James Joyce, all literature is "the eternal affirmation of man's spirit." The true poet, even the apparently obscurest, ultimately offers a simplification of the complexity that is life. According to Robert Frost, a real poem "ends in a clarification of life." The finest poetry, by means of its musicality—of the language as well as of the spirit—transports the reader into the realm of the Muse. The imagination of the true poet harmonizes the material and the spiritual, taking the reader beyond the immediate world of existence into the world of ideality. In the process, the reader undergoes some kind of a purge, forgetting the world of cares and anxieties. Perhaps it is for this reason that poets like T.S. Eliot, under the influence of the French symbolists, emphasized so much on the need for musicality of poetry. In the writings of the innumerable versifiers in India at the present time, one could notice not symphony of the human spirit but jarring cacophony of artificial words.

As examples of the trivial writing, one can cite lines like: "She is a mighty wench/who held me in her trench/kept me henpecked for long." Or, "Screams screeching we heard of men left unsheltered/Under a wild sky." Wilder than the wildest sky! An impressive rendering of thought and feeling, which is so essential to good poetry, is absent in most of these versifiers. For instance, one poet writes, "Your call/Comes to me/like a telegram/a wireless message." Another says that walking by the sea, he was "touched by the Supreme Lotion." A typical image concocted by one of these poets is worth attention: "sun a dirty coin under/muddy water." A "muddy" image indeed! Another poet writes: "They take chicken roast with/a glass of wine. Fried grams for us." It may be an authentic experience of the palate at a restaurant; but then a cookery book is perhaps a work of magnificent poetry.

Thus poetry in the hands of these innumerable poetasters fails to touch the chords of the human spirit. On the contrary, it has come to be the vocation of idlers and perverted minds vainly trying to establish a symbolic connection between the Galaxy and garbage. Freedom from the constraints of the metrical form, resulting in looseness of the verse and the haphazard choice of the subject matter has made the contemporary poetry in English banal indeed. The directness of utterance, instead of being a blessing, has become a bane to much of this writing. Meenakshi Mukherjee is right when she says that some of these poets are more fond of handling the English language than conveying a poetic vision. D.V.K. Raghavacharyulu expresses the same opinion: "A good deal of Indian poetry these days seems to be aiming at expressive strategies rather than communicative goals. Our poets purvey clippings of trendy prose as poetry." Nissim Ezekiel comes heavily on the multitude of hacks around him:

> Damn all you sensitive poets
> seducers of experience
> . . . victims of your own spontaneous fraud
> You are in hell
> and do not know it.
> When did you last write
> a real poem? ("The Company I Keep")

A major obsession of the contemporary Indian English poets seems to be with sex. Their intention might be to depict love as a primal experience. English poets like John Donne and Robert Browning have written magnificent love poetry that at once brings out the essence of the human spirit. Much of the erotic writing of the contemporary Indian poets, on the contrary, fails to reach the level of the poetry of these British poets. Nor is it anywhere near the profound love poetry of an Indian poet like Kalidasa. Perhaps these contemporary Indian poets in English are, in their anxiety to reject the devotional, what Ben Jonson in *Volpone* calls "desperate wits."

II

The "Indian reality" that Parthasarathy finds in the poetry of Ezekiel is presented in greater detail in the works of the novelists and short-story writers. Raja Rao depicts the situation of the individual in India in the metaphysical context. R.K. Narayan, with his subtle comic sense, evokes the unique atmosphere of Malgudi in his fiction. Mulk Raj Anand focuses attention on the suffering millions of India—the Bakhas of the fictional world. Bhabani Bhattacharya exposes the deceptions of the pious in the Indian society. Kamala Markandaya tries to resolve the tension between tradition and modernity, East and West, the rural and the urban. Vasant A. Shahane says: "The Indo-Anglian novel is in many ways a haphazard growth and its fortuitous development is partly the product of lack of clear objectives. An objective like the image of India or Western reader is more often a pious platitude than a genuinely realized artistic goal."[9] One has only to read the novels and short stories of the authors mentioned above to see the "image of India" presented in all its significance for the Indian and the Western reader. The three major novelists Raja Rao, R.K. Narayan, and Mulk Raj Anand together have remarkably succeeded in depicting India in both the spiritual and socio-cultural aspects. Anand's experiments in technique are well-known. It is surprising that while mentioning even Manohar Malgonkar and Kamala Markandaya as "novelists of front rank," Shahane does not care to refer to the humanist even once in the whole essay. What has been marring an accurate evaluation of the Indian novelists in English is perhaps such a critical myopia. Shahane further says: "Literary critics in their enthusiasm to win recognition for the identity of Indo-Anglian fiction have fallen an easy prey to the temptation of overrating these authors, especially novelists. In retrospect, this seems to me an avoidable critical aberration."[10] It is necessary to refer in this connection to a painstaking study of a clumsy journalistic writer like Khushwant Singh done by Shahane himself, reading into his work a basic mythical pattern and symbolic mode. Meenakshi Mukherjee finds "myth" in the Indian English novel as a structural device. While she sees such a "myth" in the works of Raja Rao and R.K. Narayan, she questions Mulk Raj Anand for the absence of it. By her own admission, however, "Anand was at the height of the power in the thirties and early forties, when a sociological approach to literature was very much in vogue in India as well as outside."[11] Well into the twenty-first century, Anand continued to be essentially a humanist in his writings. And the significance of his work for the future generation lies in the fact that he has evolved a "new myth" of the contemporary human predicament.

Taken together, the writings of the Indian English novelists cover a vaster area of the Indian reality than those of the poets. The chief interest of the novel, as Northrop Frye puts it, is in "human character as it manifests itself in society." The "human character" in India is extremely complex on account of the diversity of the Indian culture. The writings of the leading novelists like Raja Rao, R.K. Narayan, Mulk Raj Anand, Kamala Markandaya and Manohar Malgonkar, in spite of their "Indianness" in the larger sense of the term, are restricted to certain regional cultures. There are still too many aspects of the Indian life yet to be highlighted by the Indian English writers. Novelists and short-story writers in the regional languages have no doubt written at great length about these multiple regional and sub-regional cultures. The need of the hour seems to be a proliferation of fiction-writers to depict all the diversity and variety of the Indian life. Fiction, on account of the very expansive nature of the genre, is capable of presenting a sustained picture of life.

III

In his article titled "Damme, This is the Oriental Scene for You!" in *The New Yorker*, Salman Rushdie says: "The prose-writing—both fiction and non-fiction—created in this period by Indian writers working in English is proving to be a stronger and more important body of work than most of what has been produced in the eighteen 'recognized' languages of India, the so-called 'vernacular languages,' during the same time; and, indeed, this new, and still burgeoning, 'Indo-Anglian' literature represents perhaps the most valuable contribution India has yet made to the world of books. The true Indian literature of the first post-colonial half-century has been made in the language the British left behind."[12] These words, aimed at Western readership, are of a rootless expatriate Indian writer who is ignorant of the vast and complex Indian culture and literature prevailing outside Bombay. At a Sahitya Akademi seminar held in August 1998, Rushdie's assertions had been questioned by Indian intellectuals like Krishna Baldev Vaid, Namvar Singh, Keki N. Daruwalla and others. Daruwalla called him "quirky" and added that "we should spare Rushdie a kind thought, as he has been under a death threat for the past ten years. He says different things at different times to different people."[13] In "An Open Letter to Salman Rushdie" in *The Indian Express*, the well-known Bengali writer Nabaneeta Dev Sen maintained that the "article is dangerously misleading with its wealth of misinformation," and told Rushdie: "In the West, you are safe. They already know that all Indian writing is done in Sanskrit and English. But in India everyone knows Indian English is the youngest upwardly mobile literature, and is proud to share its glory. It is slightly embarrassing therefore when you brush aside other existing literary traditions from which Indians writing in English borrow. Fifty years is not much time in the history of Indian literatures."[14] The fragmented and limited Bombay vision of Rushdie is a result of his ignorance of the multiplicity of Indian subcultures contained in the treasures of what are called Bhasha literatures. The fragmentation of Rushdie's vision is also a result of his living in two worlds as an expatriate. He could not achieve what A.K. Ramanujan as an expatriate could. Ramanujan believes that "cultural traditions in India are indissolubly plural and often conflicting."[15] He is equally at home with both the Indian and American cultures. For him the American environment is the "exterior" and the Indian environment the "interior." They are the "two lobes" of his brain, as he says in an anecdote about his father.[16]

Contemporary Indian culture is extremely complex and fascinating on account of the peculiar amalgam of tradition and modernity as well as the multiplicity of subcultures and languages. The literary works, either in the regional languages or in English, are a significant means of communicating the vast variety and diversity of such a complex culture.

The Indian multiculturalism should not be viewed in the narrow perspective of what the newspapers call "fissiparous tendencies." The common factors of "Indianness" notwithstanding, each of the subcultures presents a unique value system. These local cultures are but the warp and woof of the overall fabric of the vibrant Indian society. The uniqueness of Indian culture lies in its flexibility, the overall structure remaining ever strong despite social and political upheavals and fragmentation of experience.

As Mulk Raj Anand says in his letter of December 29, 1976 to me, "Our own fiction is in the making. . . . The literatures of India will naturally have to discover the emergent human beings in novels of all kinds. . . . So far we have lived in the suspended moment of a century of struggle for freedom . . . or rather various freedoms. We are likely to replace the old myths with new tentative myths of man." What Salman Rushdie and his "children" seem to be doing is the repudiation of old Indian myths and presenting new myths of man in the postmodern times. As Anand says further, "The novel as a form matured in Europe, beyond the Indian fable, the Arab tale, and the sermons of mediaeval monks. Naturally, when we take this form from the West and adapt it to our own conditions then we have to accept a good deal of the formal approach to the novel as against our own tradition of Katha recital." Salman Rushdie and the other recent Indian English novelists are blending the oral tradition and the formal aspect of the Western novel, depicting the fragmentation of Indian life.

IV

Referring to the modern Indian English novel, Anita Desai is reported to have told an interviewer: "There is so little of it. . . . There simply isn't enough, in the name of variety, value, interest, significance."[17] However, since the 1980s, Indian English novel has taken a new turn with the publication of Salman Rushdie's *Midnight's Children* (1981). Dealing with post-Independence India in the postmodern style of fragmentation and subversion of history and myth, the fiction of the present times fuses fact and fantasy, rendered in English, coloured by words and idioms of Desi languages. This literature is able to reach out to a wider readership than the Bhasha literatures both within India and abroad on account of its advantage of being in the English language.

In Rushdie's *Midnight's Children*, the heterogeneity and fragmentation of life in Bombay would represent the state of the whole of India. As in the city of Bombay, multiculturalism and fragmentation are indicated by the frequent social and political upheavals across the country. As the narrator says at the outset of the novel, "at the precise instance of India's arrival at independence, I tumbled forth into the world. . . . I had been mysteriously handcuffed to history, my destinies chained to those of my country." Thus the history of post-Independence India and Saleem Sinai's life are inextricably connected. Rushdie resorts to what he calls "chutneyfication of history." It is subversion of history highlighting the post-Independence Indian situation. As he says, "It was as though . . . history, arriving at a point of the highest significance and promise, had chosen to sow, in that instant, the seeds of a future which would genuinely differ from anything the world had seen up to that time."[18] According to Rushdie, "It is the privilege and the curse of midnight's children to be both masters and victims of their times."[19] This state of affairs in the post-Independence India affecting the social life is also dealt with by the young Indian English novelists following Rushdie in his footsteps since the 1980s. *The New York Times* of

December 16, 1991 called these new Indian novelists "Rushdie's children."

Like Saleem Sinai of Rushdie's *Midnight's Children*, the narrator of Shashi Tharoor's novel, *The Great Indian Novel* (1989), Ved Vyas also refers to the coming of Indian Independence with "children being born at inconvenient times of the night who would go on to label a generation and rejuvenate a literature."[20] The Indian mythology of the *Mahabharata* is subverted in an attempt to show the present state of the fragmented Indian life. It is a caustic criticism of the political history of the contemporary India written in postmodern style. As Tharoor says, "*The Great Indian Novel* is an attempt to retell the political history of 20th century India through a fictional recasting of events, episodes and characters from the *Mahabharata*. . . . The *Mahabharata* has come to stand for so much in the popular consciousness of Indians: the personages in it have become household words, standing for public virtues and vices, and the issues it raises, as well as the values it seeks to promote, are central to an understanding of what makes India."[21] Tharoor takes characters and situations from the *Mahabharata* and reshapes them to tell a contemporary story, while taking liberties with the epic. He admits: "I can't see myself straying very far from the path of irreverence even in dealing with very serious subjects."[22] Ved Vyas's words to Ganapati show the reality of the post-Independence India: "No more certitudes. Accept doubt and diversity. . . . Admit there is more than one Truth, more than one Right, more than one *dharma*."[23]

Like the narrators of Rushdie's *Midnight's Children* and Tharoor's *The Great Indian Novel*, the narrator of Allan Sealy's *The Trotter-Nama* (1988) also is linked with the history of post-Independence India with its economic and social changes. In *The Trotter-Nama*, Sealy adopts the Indian method of the *nama* or chronicle, displacing the European method of historiography, presenting the history of an Anglo-Indian family in epic proportions. This is Sealy's Indian version of modernity in his belief that there are many Indian forms which may be revived and intelligently reworked. The style of presentation of history is what

Rushdie calls "chutneyfication of history." The Indian myth is presented in idealistic terms by Raja Rao in *The Serpent and the Rope* and Bhabani Bhattacharya in *A Dream in Hawaii* vis-à-vis life in the West. The younger writers of the present times resort to irreverence and subversion of the Indian myth to highlight the postmodern fragmentation of the contemporary India.

Although Salman Rushdie's vision of Indian life is largely shaped by Bombay, in *The Moor's Last Sigh* he deals with life in Kerala with its Cochin Jews and Kerala Catholics through the interaction between the Zogoiby and da Gama families. The novel also presents the spice trade of Kerala as an aspect of Indian history. Another novelist concerned with life in Kerala is Arundhati Roy who has an insider's knowledge of the subculture of the region, unlike Rushdie. Her novel *The God of Small Things* (1997), set in Ayemenem near Kottayam, relates the story of Estha and Rahel, tortured by their cruel elders Mary Kochamma, Mammachi, and Chacko who control the pickle business. The struggles of Ammu and her daughter are presented against the background of traditional Hindu narratives of disrobing of Draupadi by Dussasana and Bhima beating Dussasana in the *Mahabharata*. The novel deals with the "small God" of individual lives pitted against the "Big God" of the nation. Thus history is distorted, rewritten with reference to myth.

History and myth are dealt with by Vikram Chandra also in *Red Earth and Pouring Rain* (1995) with the overtones of fantasy. The novel tells the story of Sanjay, in the reincarnation of a monkey, stealing Abhay's new jeans. He is shot by Abhay. As Yama the god of death comes claiming the dying monkey, Ganesh enters into a deal with him that Sanjay will be saved if he can entertain everyone telling his story. Sanjay tells the story of the Indian princes and East India Company taking over the Mughal Empire. History, as the novelist says, is "The Big Indian Life," and the story is true because it is *itihasa*. It is "Leela, the great cosmic play." Thus Indian mythology is subverted and presented in postmodern terms.

In his massive novel, *A Suitable Boy* (1993), Vikram Seth reimagines the nation in epic dimensions and attempts to rewrite

Indian history. As he says, "I had written a novel set in my times in the 1980s . . . it might be interesting to explore a semi-historical terrain."[24] The novel involves a young woman Lata's quest for love in modern times. She chooses Haresh Khanna of Prahapore educated in a British technical college, instead of the Muslim Kabir Durrani and the esoteric, Amit Chatterjee. The "semi-historical terrain" involves the beginnings of the Nehru era with the first post-Independence election and the passing of the Zamindari legislation. The novel also deals with communal riots and politics and violence involving college students.

Amitav Ghosh is certainly the best among the new novelists writing in the style of Rushdie. A gifted craftsman, Ghosh deals with India's place in international culture. As A.K. Ramanujan says, "he evokes things Indian with an inwardness that is lit and darkened by an intimacy with Elsewhere." In his first novel, *The Circle of Reason* (1986), Ghosh deals with India's tradition of cultural exchange with the West, from rural Bengal to the Gulf states and Egypt. *The Shadow Lines* (1988) depicts the Datta-Chaudhuri family displaced from Dhaka to Calcutta after the Partition. The self and the nation are in conflict, involving cultural identity. *The Calcutta Chromosome* (1996), written in postmodern style, presents the interaction of science, history and colonialism. In all his works, Ghosh renders a cultural matrix in the context of India as a fragmented nation.

Another recent novelist dealing with conflict between tradition and modernity in India is Upamanyu Chatterjee. His novel, *English, August: An Indian Story* (1988) presents the protagonist Agastya (called "August" by his friends) as rootless and culturally dislocated as a man of the new generation, the "generation of apes" and an "absurd combination of . . . a boarding-school-English literature education and an obscure name from Hindu myths." The sage Agastya moved the Vindhyas, but the bureaucrat August fails to move the mountain of inefficiency and corruption. As Chatterjee says, the novel is "a cult book" in which "the urban, English-speaking Indian has been put on the literary map." Chatterjee's *The Last Burden* (1993) presents the conflicts among urban Indian families. He is a great chronicler of the Indian middle class reduced to a minority status in modern times with no government benefits.

The multiple languages and subcultures in India cannot remain unaffected by external influences. In fact, the interaction between the Indian languages and English is growing in modern times. As Upamanyu Chatterjee says in *English, August: An Indian Story*, "Amazing mix. . . . Hazaar fucked. Urdu and American. . . . I'm sure nowhere else could language be mixed and spoken with ease." English is used in different ways in different regions of the country with varying mix of the regional tang. With its unique position in the contemporary Indian culture, English is ingrained with the polyphony of Indian languages. In *Midnight's Children*, Salman Rushdie "chutneyfies" English, mixing up Urdu or Hindi words with the English. The main problem before the Indian writer in English is to convey the specifically Indian feelings and thought processes in a foreign medium. As Raja Rao says, "Our method of expression, therefore, has to be a dialect which will some day prove to be as distinctive and colourful as the Irish or the American. Time alone will justify it."[26] Indian English has certainly acquired a respectable status of its own as a dialect of English acceptable to the international community. In the words of R.K. Narayan, "Bharat English will respect the rule of law and maintain the dignity of grammar, but still have a Swadeshi stamp about it unmistakably, like the Madras handloom check shirt or the Tirupathi doll."[27] Mulk Raj Anand tries to naturalize the alien language by literal translation of Hindi or Punjabi idiom into English. As he puts it, "I generally translate or interpret my feelings or thoughts from Punjabi or Hindustani into the English language, thus translating the metaphor or imagery of my mother tongue into what is called Indo-Anglo-Indian writing, but what I prefer to call 'pigeon-Indian' (not Pidgin-Indian)."[28] Raja Rao, R.K. Narayan, and Mulk Raj Anand could achieve Indianization of English in their writings highlighting not only the pan-Indian culture but also the specific subcultures of Kannada, Hindustani, and Punjabi.

NOTES

1. Adil Jussawalla, *New Writing in India* (New Delhi: Penguin, 1974) 34.
2. R. Parthasarathy, "How it Strikes a Contemporary: The Poetry of A.K. Ramanujan," *The Literary Criterion* (Special Number on Indian Writing in English), XII, Nos. 2-3 (1976):188.
3. Mulk Raj Anand, "Trends in the Modern Indian Novel," *The Journal of Indian Writing in English*, I, i (January 1973) 5.
4. Adil Jussawalla, "The New Poetry," *Readings in Commonwealth Literature*, ed. William Walsh (New Delhi: Oxford University Press, 1973) 76.
5. R. Parthasarathy, ed., *Ten Twentieth-Century Indian Poets* (New Delhi, 1976) 95-96.
6. Shiv K. Kumar, "A Letter from New York," *Subterfuges* (New Delhi, 1976) 22.
7. Walt Whitman, "As I Ebb'd with the Ocean of Life," *Walt Whitman: Representative Selections*, ed. Floyd Stovall (New York, 1934) 183.
8. Review of A. Viswam's *River My Guru*, *The Journal of Indian Writing in English*, II, ii (July 1974) 65.
9. Vasant A. Shahane, "Indo-English Fiction and the Question of Form," *The Journal of Indian Writing in English*, *Ibid.*, 35.
10. *Ibid.*
11. M. Mukherjee, *The Twice-Born Fiction* (New Delhi, 1971) 78.
12. Salman Rushdie, "Damme, This is the Oriental Scene for You!" *The New Yorker* (June 23 & 30, 1997): 50.
13. "In Salman's Shadow," *The Indian Express*, August 13, 1998.
14. *The Indian Express*, July 13, 1997.
15. A.K. Ramanujan, *The Critical Essays of A.K. Ramanujan*, ed. Vinay Dharwadkar (New Delhi: Oxford University Press, 1999) 8.
16. *The Critical Essays*, 36.
17. Atma Ram, *Interviews with Indo-English Writers* (Calcutta: Writers Workshop, 1983)
18. Salman Rushdie, *Midnight's Children* (New York: Avon Books, 1982) 215.
19. *Ibid.*, 552.
20. Shashi Tharoor, *The Great Indian Novel* (New Delhi: Penguin India, 1989) 239.

21. "Yoking of Myth to History," *Littcrit*, Vol. 16, Nos. 1-2 (June-December 1990) 5.
22. "Writers at Work: Shashi Tharoor interviewed by Anjali Mathur," *Gentleman*, Vol. 10, No. 1 (1990): 54.
23. Shashi Tharoor, *The Great Indian Novel*, 418.
24. "The Novel of Our Times," *The Hindustan Times*, 27 February 1993: 4.
25. "On the Road," *The Times of India*, 22 November 1992: 5.
26. Raja Rao, *Kanthapura* (1938; Madras: Oxford University Press, 1963) v-vi
27. R.K. Narayan, *Reluctant Guru* (Delhi, 1974) 57.
28. "'Pigeon-Indian': Some Notes on Indian-English Writing," Seminar on Australian and Indian Literature, New Delhi, January 12-16, 1970: 8.

Mulk Raj Anand

Bombay
December 17, 1976

Dear Friend,

I was going to say young friend, but I am afraid, that you might think, I am being patronising.

As an obedient servant of all new talents, I have given some thought to your questionnaire.

I felt that, in the first instance, I must put down a preliminary note about my attitude so that the context in which I may answer the questionnaire would be the framework of India today. I mean by this that I do not consider much European literary criticism to be relevant to the novels in India, whether they are in the Indian-English or in the various languages of our country. From within the texture of the new writings, critical values will arise eventually. As you know, people like Henry James, Percy Lubbock and even Forster were from different social milieu than all of us.

Only our university education has been mainly in terms of English literary criticism so far as literature is concerned. And all the observations of Goethe, Schiller, Lunaharsky, Gide, Benda Lukac and Sartre have been ignored. The continentals were far more aware of the connection between life and literature, because of the French revolution, and later the revolt against art for art's sake followed the Symbolist movement. Arthur Rimbaud blew all the literary men sky high, like soap bubbles, from North France before the age of eighteen and wrote entirely from the love of the landscape of the Ardennes.

I will also send you later some of my articles on the novel, which I wrote occasionally for seminars.

With kindliest wishes,

Yours sincerely,
Mulk Raj Anand

P.S.: I could send you the MSS of my lectures, but this is unrevised. And perhaps as a *quid pro quo* for my work in answer to your questionnaire, you could look through the text of my lectures and pencil suggestion, emendations and revisions beyond the type-script errors. If you promise that, I will send it to you.

* * * * *

Warangal
December 25, 1976

Dear Dr. Anand,

Greetings to you for 1977!

I'm grateful to you for your very affectionate note of December 17 and the enclosed "Preliminary General Answer" to my questionnaire concerning your art of fiction. I look forward to receiving your specific answers. Kindly do send me the mss. of your lectures ("Novel Form in the Ocean of Story"). I'll take notes from those lectures with all your emendations, marginalia, etc. and return the stuff to you if you insist. I would like to attempt a comprehensive article on your idea (if not "theory") of fiction. This is the kind of study I have done in my recently completed Ph.D. thesis on Poe's fictional theory and practice.

Perhaps at this stage of my life it's difficult to have full control over what is surging from the depths of my being. It's this fascinating experience that has prompted me to have an extended dialogue with you, but no schoolboy-like "academic" enthusiasm. While trying to be objective, I tend to be somewhat subjective too, trying to discover myself through my exchanges with you.

Both your theory and practice are certainly beyond the ken of the "Ignoramuses" like that great South Indian cynic you refer to, who, with a limited knowledge, pass judgement on others with Johnsonian authority. However, I think you should give some allowance to those senior Professors who are "Professors" only to earn their bread (a very social problem), sometimes unpredictable in their literary judgement, but who are kindred souls with creative inclinations.

I think a writer's "theory" gradually evolves from his practice itself. He needn't write a "Professional thesis," as you put it, in order to state what he is going to say in his creative work. In other words, there will be a constant back and forth movement on the part of the writer—looking at what he has already accomplished and what more he has to say and how he has to say that. In this connection it is interesting to consider the theory of "intention" that has caused a storm in the teacup for theorists and aestheticians. W.K. Wimsatt and Monroe Beardsley, while admitting that there are two kinds of intention, i.e., "internal evidence" (the text itself) and the "external evidence" (letters, prefaces, etc.) maintain that "the design or intention of the author is neither available nor desirable as a standard for judging the success of a work of literary art." However, Ananda K. Coomaraswamy seems to me to be convincing when he asserts, in answer to Wimsatt and Beardsley, that there are two kinds of inquiry about a work of art: (1) whether the artist achieved his intentions; (2) whether the work of art "aught ever to have been undertaken at all" and so whether it is worth preserving." I think these are the considerations that should prompt a proper assessment of the achievement of a literary artist. Without some kind of an intention the writer cannot improve upon what he has done.

In the third paragraph of your covering letter, you say that European literary criticism is irrelevant to the novels of India because writers like Henry James and Forster wrote in a different social milieu. In the next paragraph you maintain that continentals like Goethe, Schiller, Gide, and Sartre are more relevant to us because of their awareness of life and literature. While accepting this premise, we should perhaps consider the basic connection between life and literature as having been given an artistic shape in their writing (whether that deals with the caste system, the class conflict or just the family relationships). In depicting these human relationships, the writer resorts to certain compositional methods in an attempt to create an illusion of (social) life. If this is not done, I think there is no difference between creative writing and journalism. In other words, taking the physical (social) reality, the novelist or the short story writer attempts to fictionalise that reality by means of character, incident, dialogue, and atmosphere. I think, in this sense it matters little whether a writer is depicting the European society or the Indian society, whether he is concerned with the so-called "democracy" or with the so-called 'communism." I will be grateful if you could kindly enlighten me on this aspect of your fictional art.

Once again, I'm grateful to you for your very thoughtful answers to my questions.

With warm regards,

Yours sincerely,
D. Ramakrishna

* * * * *

Some Queries to Dr. Mulk Raj Anand

I. Henry James, in his famous essay, "The Art of Fiction," maintains, while disagreeing with Walter Besant in respect of the didactic fiction, that a novelist is close to a philosopher and painter. At several places you have described the novelist as a poet. Do you agree with James and maintain that the novelist is a "painter" of life? After all, technically, there are affinities between the poet and the painter. As James puts it, "Do not think too much about optimism and pessimism; try and catch the color of life itself." How far do you agree with such a view?

II. Sir Walter Scott says in *Lives of the Poets* that every successful novelist must be more or less a poet in that he feels acutely and that "his accurate power of examining and embodying human character and human passion, as well as the external face of nature" is similar to the poet's. Is this view similar to your own conception of the novel as a poem? Or is it only Wilfred Owen's "Poetry is in the Pity" that you have in mind?

III. When I read your works dealing with the squalor of life, I am reminded of the massive writing of the great American novelist Theodore Dreiser. Dreiser was fascinated by Communism and for a while joined the Communist Party of Russia, having visited that country. But later, he got disillusioned with that ideology because of his basically humanist attitude. These philosophical attitudes have had a considerable effect on the technique of Dreiser's fictional writing which tends to be massive. Do you agree with me if I maintain that both in theme and technique your writing resembles Dreiser's? If Dreiser's work does not deal with the "untouchable" in the sense of being a Harijan, it certainly describes the outcast of the twentieth-century industrialized America. I think to some extent you universalize the experience of the untouchable.

IV. You say in your letter to Saros Cowasjee dated the 5th of July, 1968: "Pity, I think my stories are better than most of my novels. I can concentrate on the finesse and the craftsmanship. Also they reflect many more obscure existences than a novel does or can." This is almost what Edgar Allan Poe, the nineteenth-century American tale-writer says. According to Poe, the tale is preferable to the novel because of its brevity and unity of effect. The novel, like the long poem, he maintains, is a contradiction in terms. Also the tale, on account of the intensity and brevity of the effect on the reader's sensibility, is lyrical. Do you aim at such a lyrical effect in your short stories? You say in your letter to Saros Cowasjee of the 7th of September, 1970 that the novel form is "loose." Do you prefer the tale (or the short story) to the novel for the compactness of the form?

V. In your letter to Cowasjee dated the 7th of Sept. 1970 you barely refer to "communication" with reference to the novel. Will you please elaborate on the idea of communication that is in your mind while writing? Do you write primarily to "communicate" or to produce an "effect" or just to document a social idea?

VI. In your letter to Cowasjee dated the 22nd of November, 1967, you refer to the author-narrator relationship, saying that in your work, "the characters take charge." Also you insist upon "distance" as an essential concept. Do you then believe in the "dramatic novel"?

You say, in the same letter, that "the novelist should try to become the great God, Brahma. . . ." Elsewhere you show preference for the first-person narration. (Your conversation with Marlene fisher, quoted in Marlene Fisher, "Mulk Raj Anand's confessional Novels," *The Journal of Indian Writing in English*, Vol. 14, No. 2 (July, 1976): 41) Which of the forms do you largely use in your writing?

VII. In your letter to Cowasjee dated the 5th of August 1968, you refer to Percy Lubbock's *The Craft of Fiction*, saying that it is superior to E.M. Forster's *Aspects of the Novel*. In fact, Wayne C. Booth's *The Rhetoric of Fiction* (1961) is more comprehensive, elaborating on the numerous fictional aspects dealt with by Lubbock. As Professor Booth puts it,

> The success of an author's rhetoric does not depend on whether he thought about his readers as he wrote; if 'mere calculation' cannot insure success, it is equally true that even the most unconscious and Dionysian of writers succeeds only if he makes us join in the dance. (Preface to *The Rhetoric of Fiction*)

Do you, as a writer of fiction, aim at producing an effect on the reader? Is your theory mimetic?

VIII. There is obviously some controversy concerning your use of the technique of stream of consciousness. However, in some of your letters to Cowasjee and to Paul Verghese you refuse to be identified with the Joycean school. While reading *Morning Face*, I have come across a passage which has interested me. Krishan exclaims:

> Let me dedicate myself to that disordered imagination of the new poetry beyond insipid harmonious rhymes, or passions sung and understood by the singer, away from pastimes, full of pain and ineffable torture and the utterest joy, not only in hexameters, but in the rich flow of words, like a river." (*Morning Face*)

In your letter to Saros Cowasjee dated the 20th of December, 1969, referring to truth, you say Thomas Wolfe is concerned with telling it. And then you refer to *Morning Face*. You know well that Thomas Wolfe, in telling the truth, is concerned with the theory of time and the river—the stream of consciousness—wherein also there is "the rich flow of words, like a river." (to quote from *Morning Face*). What do you think of Wolfe's *Of Time and the River*?

You frequently refer to the "amorphousness" of the novel form. Do you think that brings you close to the Wolfean concept?

In your letter to Saros Cowasjee dated November 1971, you say:

> Perhaps it is because of the inner power of the dark encounter, in spite of the nightmarish *Finnegans Wake* quality of the writing in this novel, that quite a few critics go to it. (*The Big Heart*)

About *The Road* you say in your letter to Saros Cowasjee dated the 12th of December 1971:

> I, therefore, pursued the mirror game, at various levels of consciousness of the people, concave and convex, involved in this drama of the soul. You will notice that, technically, it is not a straight narrative, but diversified by breaking through the obvious planes to the impalpable world of feelings of the characters involved.

Do you think that this "mirror game" contributes to the poetic aspect of your fiction? Has your poetry in this respect got something to do with the stream of consciousness too? Kindly enlighten me on this crucial issue.

D. Ramakrishna

* * * * *

Bombay
December 29, 1976

Dear Shri Ramakrishna,

In the midst of preparations to go to Delhi for various meetings, including the Commonwealth Writers Conference, I received your note of December 25th.

I was in the midst of *Marg* research into Pahari Painting all this week, in order to see the Lahore Museum Collection, when I go there, if I go there, in January. So I am afraid, your questionnaire has remained unanswered.

I will answer it, though, I feel, from the point of view of any reflections by an Indian novelist on the novel, the references to the various critics of novels abroad will not help very much.

Our own fiction is in the making. The general appellation is likely to be the novel of humanism, because we are discovering our love of man for the first time in 2000 years outside the established dharma.

The literatures of India will naturally have to discover the emergent human beings in novels of all kinds. And the criticism of the theories of criticism about these fictions will arise from internal developments.

So far as the practice of the few writers with an opus, Mr. Narayan refuses to say very much, Raja Rao has almost abandoned novel writing for the Advaita, and I am the only sinner who goes on in the belief that, ultimately, each one of us must knock our souls on the smithy of our consciences and recreate the truth, beauty and tenderness from the sources of love which are in our people.

Incidental to this kind of creative work are the technical devices which we might originate, borrow and adapt to suit the human predicament in our civilisation.

So far we have lived in the suspended moment of a century of struggle for freedom—or rather various freedoms. We are likely to replace the old myths with new tentative myths of man. We have to see our displacements, our repudiation of the tribe, our wanderings, exaltations and agonies of aloneness, the heartbreaks, the furies, the ribaldry, the phantoms, neither heroic nor hopeful, neither high-minded nor low-minded, in the dailiness which is the working hypothesis of our tenancies on earth. All these may turn out to be the realities, dreams and nightmares, which European writers faced for 200 years more, and our metaphysical yearnings are incipiently anti-heroic.

No one writer can do all the necessary things. And as the confrontation of all the realities has to be total, we will fail. But our failure will have shown the way to others.

Therefore, these formulations must not depart beyond *human relations*, that is the one thing I have learnt from the West, especially from Morgan Forster.

I am unable to trace the MSS of the lectures which are in Khandala. At any rate, I couldn't have sent these to you in this haste, because even the typing errors are not corrected. I will do so in the New Year.

With very warm regards,

Yours sincerely,
Mulk Raj Anand

* * * * *

Bombay
January 21, 1977

Dear Friend,

Always when I return from an excursion away from office, there is a huge wad of correspondence waiting for me and the dailiness of life reduces one to pulp, so that it is not possible to do any imaginative work.

Anyhow, I have had your questionnaire in mind which is really an order to write a book. I gave one note to a colleague in answer to the first point of your questionnaire, so I am sending that to you in the hope that I will have time, slowly, to answer the next point this weekend.

I am not sure where I am contradicting myself. Maybe I am. And to that I have only Walt Whitman's answer.

I must look up the letter you refer to. I may have talked of Flaubert as against Tolstoy and commented on the quarrel between Percy Lubbock and E.M. Forster. That vital difference of opinion is important to all discussions of the novel, even when we evolve our own *obiter dicta*. There are certain universal propositions on which one cannot have a sectional point of view. Anyhow the novel as a form matured in Europe, beyond the Indian fable, the Arab tale, and sermons of mediaeval monks. Naturally, when we take this form from the West and adapt it to our own conditions then we have to accept a good deal of the formal approach to the novel as against our own tradition of Katha recital.

I would beg you not to take me too literally. I am not attempting a theory of the novel, as I told you. I am only putting down certain hunches or reflections from within the practice of the novel form, in a broken age, from within a country where there are so many hangovers of confusion.

I am trying to record, recreate or insinuate, certain hints about the philosophy of criticism which might be possible in the context of fragmented societies like ours, where the novel as epic in the Homeric sense is not possible. The breakdown of everything in our age, and more than the breakdown the dispersal of cultures, leaves no room for coherent theories or for harmonious writing; only confrontations of the miscellaneous realities are possible.

I don't know if I am able to communicate my meaning. You may have to imagine much of what I have no time to put down. For instance, how can I analyse for you our prolonged existentialism coming from the centuries of Advaita? In what way shall I bridge the gulf that divides those who are resigned to despair to those who want to live and read books and cultivate the sensibility? Every time I address such a question to myself, I find all our professors or almost all, trying to find the mysticism behind the man standing on the leg in R.K. Narayan's novel, or discover in the rope the serpent power. Or seek oblivion in the blind alleys of the torn sensibility of Anita Desai, Nayantara Sahgal and Ruth Jhabvala. But let me not be impatient until after I answer your questionnaire.

About the lectures on the novel, I am afraid I will not have any time until the Spring, to look at the MSS. If you can undertake the typescript, typed by a young Parsi girl, who does not know anything about Rama and Sita, and calls Bankim Bunkum, then I will send it to you, and, as a *quid pro quo*, you can revise the text for me or do pencillings. I will then have a text which I want to revise anyhow finally. But I am frightened of the critics who might tend to consider an unrevised MSS as sheer bad writing.

More later.

Regards.

Yours sincerely,
Mulk Raj Anand

Henry James and the Art of Fiction

Henry James began writing his comments on fiction at a time when there was a bitter controversy going on, in the world of Visual Arts. There were those like Whistler and Oscar Wilde, who had borrowed the idea of art for art's sake from late 19th century France. And there were those like Ruskin and Morris, who believed that art served some purpose, insofar as beauty was an essential part of objects used in everyday life and helped men and women to cultivate finer feelings. As an expatriate from America, the provincial Henry James wished to be eligible to the world of pure form in the manner of Flaubert's *Madame Bovary*. But as his theme was derived from the raw material of the newly emergent American middle class, he was constrained to bring in insidious conflicts due to stress of cash nexus, into his narratives. Also he made comments beyond Flaubert's pure telling of the tale. And he asserted that the novelist is often closer to a philosopher.

It is true that James' philosophy of life is more implicit in the development of his characters and situations, insofar as they show preference for one way of life or another. But the novel form being, in our tragic age inevitabiy loose (because it has to take in the background), he could not be the detached novelist that was Flaubert.

In fact, none of his contemporaries in America, as well as Thomas Hardy and Joseph Conrad, could be pure aesthetes. They were all compelled to present life under the overall influence of the predicaments of the new middle class, produced by the Industrial Revolution. And, however much he tried to emphasise the "colour of life" and to avoid "optimism and pessimism, "quite a few of his characters show negative attitudes. He does not share the pessimism of Thomas Hardy, but he has not much hope for the Americans either.

The problems faced by Henry James, Joseph Conrad, and Thomas Hardy are vastly different from the predicament of man in India in the 20th century, when our people have struggled for freedom, when there have been two world wars and preparations for a third one are going on. Besides, the texture of the world has been changed by the Russian and the Chinese revolutions. And the world is divided between the affluent peoples of the West and the newly emergent poor peoples of two thirds of the world in bitter conflicts of ideas, emotions and feelings, of those who are still not free from racial discrimination and wish to emerge from the labyrinths to attain human dignity.

Under these conditions, the novelist is constrained not merely to be a dispassionate observer of the fates but to be a philosopher committed to life against death. He has to make a total confrontation of the suspended moment of liberation of our century, and to see every situation in this tragic period from the point of view of how the urges of his characters for political freedom, and the other implied freedom, can be expressed within the context of the art form of the novel.

Of course, he must catch the "colour of life" itself, or its vitality, in all its ebb and flow. But, when the "unknown fate," which is the new god of money and power hangs over the heads of all the characters, in all parts of the world, the clouds of war become denser, and the threat of the extinction of our planet looms large, the sombre atmosphere is bound to induce melancholy in the soul; the colours of life are almost dimmed into the ashen grey of death.

Actually, the existentialist despair has affected most serious novelists of the West. The "fear and trembling" of Kierkegaard has possessed not only Camus and Sartre, but also Beckett and Ionesco.

If in the Afro-Asian world there have appeared men like Premchand, Sarat Chatterjee, Lu Hsun, Sholokov and Ichikawa, who go beyond despair to some hope, it is because the human struggle for liberation imbues characters with the vitality of life impulses.

So, James's advice, "not to think too much about optimism and pessimism" is the advice of a smug bourgeois, who had an independent income and could afford to be complacent about the grim realities of the struggle between the two nations in the Britain of his time.

Joseph Conrad, whom James admired, and Thomas Hardy went much deeper and embraced wider horizons. And although both these and many others seem to have felt that the "colour of life" is not possible, as in Homer's epic of the early Greek period, their efforts at total confrontation of many characters and situations and feelings enabled them to face the displacement of human beings through the cash nexus society, the wanderings of their heroes in search of the "heart of darkness," the agonies of loneliness, and betrayal of man by man, the heart-breaks of women—thus recreating insights which come from poetry and the courage of the novelist to ally himself intensely with all his characters.

Indeed Thomas Hardy even attempted the self-conscious epic called the *Dynasts*, which failed because broken age could not make for harmony in poetry.

If we accept that in our time the harmony of the age of the Gods is not possible, we can produce bits and pieces of the loose epic novel, which may be conducive to integration by piling up insights, from the wisdom of the heart, and these insights themselves may add up the evolution of men and women.

We have, however, in our newly emergent societies to understand that we are not the middle classes of Europe and America. We must see ourselves as we are. We are struggling out of the caste orders, emancipating our minds from the submission to one-man rule, we are dimly becoming aware of our resignation to the unknown fate. The Supreme God Vishnu will not wake up to help us because the *Kaliyug* is not yet over. We are still going through the various seasons of hell brought by the Christian idea of suffering which submerged our pagan impulses. We have inherited a racial unconscious which, though accepted the warning of the Buddha about pain as the inevitable undertone of life, still resists existentialism from the sheer vitality of the folk acceptance of the cosmos.

We cannot, therefore, accept the novel of the Western bourgeois in its totality even though we accept the form of the novel evolved by the middle classes for the middle classes.

We have to reveal the new consciousnesses of our old-new peoples, in all their miscellaneousness, in the imaginative portrayal of human life that is the novel.

And in the uncharted seas into which we adventure, we have to evolve new instruments for navigation—that is to say, we have to define new tests for judging whether we are on the right track to wherever we are going.

General Answer to Questionnaire

Apropos your Questionnaire on my Theory of Fiction

Those people who say I have no theory of fiction are more or less correct. And yet one does not need to formulate a systematic theory to love fiction and react to its various expressions, to enjoy its flavours and even to write some creative criticism of one's own. So I have certain hunches about the novel but have not put these down in any book or formal essay. I have jotted down several reflections. And these Sutra-like notes can be offered instead of a professional thesis or theory of fiction.

I delivered some lectures entitled "A Novel Form in the Ocean of Story" in the Panjab University, in which I have put down a number of comments on the Katha recitals of the first two thousand years of our literature, as against the attempted novels of the modern period, from Bankim Chatterjee downwards. The freedom of the spoken word appeals to me, because in the casual remark, or an aside, one may say something significant, which is deadened by theorising on paper. And I am putting down a few stray thoughts below from which my attitudes may come through.

Although we in India owe a good deal to the European or rather English novel, from the 18th century downwards, I think we have, by and large, emergent among us, a new kind of form, shaped by our various habits of thought, our conscious and subconscious inheritance, speech, symbols and images, tested by our present-day living realities, as against the Katha recital or sermon-fictions of the past. I feel that our modern writings cannot integrate the ancient Dharmic lessons, because we have been transplanted into the world of human sympathy through the emphasis on human relations between individuals under conditions of the many struggles for freedom in the transition from the age of one-man-rule to participatory democracy.

The arrival of the individual in the 20th century has introduced the conflicts of the *Kaliyug* as against the supposed harmonies of the *Satyug*. Vishnu Bhagwan went to sleep in the coils of the Sheshnag. And he will not wake up until the dawn of the new age of truth, an age which will never arrive, because we are surging forward to so many freedoms which the various world revolutions have brought including hopes of a millenium of the mutual aid society. Of course, the utopia will never arrive, because the very freedom of conscience, which men and women longed for, is baulked by the hangovers of the past prohibitions and the impositions of new inhibitions, but certainly the life of the individual is in the process of change. The zigzag of evolution always sparks off stagnant societies, the quick of which sets off various transformation and metamorphosis, followed by conservation and again to the struggles against slavery of mind and body.

Underneath these processes the renewal of the individual, through confrontation of reality, compels human beings to renew themselves.

But evolution has to be conscious of itself if we are not vegetables.

And consciousness becomes the highest ideal of the awakening individual.

The renewal is not an obvious or pre-determined Karmic process. It is a kind of evolutionary dialectic of conflicts, oppositions and labyrinthine rhythmic interplay and may possibly result in synthesis, through experience of life at various levels, in different situations.

Sometimes those who are in the process of awakening put down their remembrances and achieve some beauty of expression so that we may contemplate the inner and outer currents which flow in their creative writings.

The novel is one form of recreation of our flow in time, the refreshing river, with its many waves, eddies, enrushes and whirlpools and deep insinuations.

In this sense, the flow of the river of a novel assumes a form, through which several lives may be crystallized into characters, revealing fundamental urges, obscure imperceptible feelings and intensely impassioned thoughts, which may give discreet pleasures or yield some meaning, or define a mood, or several moods and emotions from unreasoned beliefs to ignorance, delusion and fantasy.

If we ask ourselves what happens when we read a novel, or rather after we have read it, we will find strange evocations in ourselves. The general atmosphere may become a kind of aura in which we may live and move and have our being, as we do after reading Tolstoy's *War and Peace*. Or we may be possessed by a character, or a number of characters, like the Brothers Karamazov. Or we may be startled into the consciousness of an important event like the end of Tess in Thomas Hardy's *Tess of the d'Urbervilles*. Perhaps some of the exploits in Dandin's *Ten Princes* may affect us. I have found myself being very susceptible to the idea of tilting imaginary windmills as in *Don Quixote*. It is possible that we may enrich our conversation by recounting the gossip about the Americans in a novel by Henry James. Maybe the battle of ideas in Andre Gide's *The Counterfeiters* may fascinate us by the subtle interplay of oppositions between honest truths and clever phrases. Perhaps the sea rich for wholeness of James Joyce in *Ulysses* may come through, if we struggle through the streams of consciousness of Mr. & Mrs. Bloom and Stephen Daedalus. Or we may begin to feel the nuances of feeling of Virginia Woolf's *Mrs. Dalloway*, as she walks along the

Thames embankment. All kinds of stirrings are possible. And the residuum of the whole remains in a variegated assortment of feelings in our own life, which may refine our sensibility and sustain us in the constant struggle to cultivate themselves and live more intensely.

No critic can reproduce the essence of a novel, through neat little theories of realism, subjectivism, naturalism, social realism or anti-novel novel metaphysics about love, jealousy or contempt. Because the novel is generally a whirlpool, in which we get involved, and go round and round, being unable to extricate ourselves, unless someone pulls us out, as the wife does by saying: "The dinner is getting cold."

All that really happens to us on plunging into the whirlpool of a significant novel is then difficult to analyse. But somehow or the other, through the impact of a great book, our life may be changed, ever so slightly, as a river changes its course occasionally through the pressure of the elements. Or we may be moved to sympathy and feel, inside us, a tremor which the heroine felt. Or our emotions may be changed. Or we may confirm our familiar feelings, saying, "I felt like that also!" Therefore, we must be cautious in delivering judgements about novels from the high pedestals of our authoritative positions as professors of literature.

The criticism of the novel may be more meaningful, if we try to understand the creative process, through which the author unfolds his experiences of the passions and the acts of his characters in a plausible enough form which may communicate the totality of his preoccupations to the reader.

The alliance of the critic (who is an intelligent reader) with a novel can only come from a creative criticism and not from external *obiter-dicta*, enunciated either by Henry James, Percy Lubbock or E.M Forster—though the last mentioned critic was far more tentative in putting forward hypotheses and called himself a "pseudo-scholar." The novel does not admit the kind of dictatorial assertions, for or against, of some Shivaramakrishna.

It is possible that D.H. Lawrence was instinctively correct when he asked for the flow of sympathy as a way of appreciation of the novel. Antipathy does not give a chance to show the ambiguities which may be in a novel. And prejudice deforms judgement.

This does not mean, however, that one should be vague, loose and white-livered in projecting oneself into a novel. If the book does not stir us, by its own momentum, or "bounce" as Morgan Forster calls it, or the "spark" as I would like to call it, organically, then I feel the novel in question is as dead as Dodo.

I cannot indicate any method to probe the mysteries of human life in a novel beyond this kind of alliance. Only I can suggest a few precautions against bias.

First of all one must not think that the whole novel form is exhausted by the classics of European literature and the several million novels in the West. There is no truth in the phrase of the classroom that the novel form finished with *Ulysses*. I would like to say that, in fact, *Ulysses* released the novel form to the vital experiences of millions of other consciousnesses than those of Mr. & Mrs. Bloom or Stephen Daedalus. There are going to be many novels beyond the accepted classics, the acknowledged books, and the second or third rate commercial narratives.

May I venture to suggest that each life in the human world is different from the other and lends itself to confrontation in its tragi-comedy, within the milieu in which the individual lives, the peculiar moods by which he is possessed and the vicarious indulgences of the lonely, helpless and forlorn wanderer, which is the human heart.

There may be some approximation in the new novels to the classics of the past. But we must not mistake the old novels for Bibles. Always the past works prepare the way for the present and the future. The new novels, by virtue of the word, "Novel," which means new, are fresh upturnings of the soil in which new flowers may grow. There are no symbols which are inherently poetical. There are no forms which can last forever. Only perhaps, the fundamentals of human life are eternal—life itself, love, pain, hatred, jealousy, desire and the longings for light against darkness.

In the struggle for the novel of the new consciousness, of new heroes and heroines, new situations and new passions, everything changes.

I am, then, for the novel of the new consciousness.

There is no doubt that any single human life on our planet, which is part of many galaxies, is a flower which will grow and then fall away, after it has faced the sun and then been assailed by Yama.

But, to the extent to which the human being is a flower, and is able to become aware of his growth, the joys of the earth remain sweet, the sorrows remain bitter, and love is shared, from the moment the child is suckled on the breast to the time when man mates with woman, and in the many moments when the light enters the dim areas of the soul.

Of course, human life always faces the question mark of death.

The Greeks wanted to hasten death, as when Oedipus cries like Job: "Perish the man whoever he was, who freed me in the pastures from the cruel shackles on my feet, and saved me from death, and gave me back to life. Oh! Thankless deed! Had I died then to my friends and to my known soul, I had not been so sore a grief."

The ancient Indians thought of death differently. They did not consider the passions of love, hate and pride as blind forces, like the Greeks, but as part of human nature which is transitory and not all suffering. It is true that Buddha felt that life was all Dukha. But the concept of the world as *lila*, play, was accepted by the Hindus above the deep frustrations, separations, banishments and suspended living between something and something.

In the refulgence of desire, in the love play, in smiles and tears, in the recurrence of good and bad, in beauty married by ugliness in the conflicts of the elements, we are part of the flow of Time and refreshing river. In our culture the dance of Shiva symbolises the forces of creation, preservation and dissolution, and the daily release of the rhythm to achieve poise.

It is likely therefore that in the miscellaneousness of existence, in all its dailiness, in its exaltations and despairs, we are tied to the life in the here and the now, in the flesh and the blood, in all its human implications. In every heart we breathe is the urge for a fresh breath.

Mulk Raj Anand

* * * * *

Bombay
February 18, 1977

Dear Friend,

As I anticipated, I could not get down to any part of your long questionnaire beyond what I have answered. If you look at your copy of the questionnaire, you will find that it would take a few months to answer it. At least a whole week of self-absorption, with a good Secretary to take notes down. In the present situation when I am trying to stabilise the publishing house of Art, *Marg*, which I founded 30 years ago, it may be difficult to get that much time until the late Spring, but then I am due to go to Pakistan for *Marg* research.. And, on my return, I will have the fourth volume of my long novel to revise for press.

I think, therefore, that, if you will forgive the rawest raw material of my Tagore lectures as an answer to some questions of yours, you might be able to glean some information, explicit or implicit, about by attitude to the novel form in our country today. I say today, because I don't know what I shall say tomorrow when some of our bright young people will have adopted the point of view of the anti-novel-novel.

May I emphasise that what I am sending you are my notes towards the lectures, differentiating roughly the bardic recital from the novel *quo* novel.

If during your perusal you find yourself pencilling it ruthlessly, or at least making crosses on the margin by way of questions, alterations, revisions, event typing errors, I shall be grateful when I come to revise the book for the Panjab University, who want to see it in press, as soon as possible.

I am going off to Goa for a week and will be in Bombay till about 12th March when I go to Delhi enroute to Pakistan.

With kindliest wishes,

Yours sincerely,

Mulk Raj Anand

* * * * *

Warangal
April 9, 1997

Dear Dr. Anand,

I trust that you have got my letter of February 28 acknowledging receipt of your manuscript on *A Novel Form in the Ocean of Story*. I find the thing a very interesting reading, being creative criticism of the first order. Only, it does smack of lecture notes. Now that I have completed teaching work for the semester, I am closely reading the ms. I have undertaken the task as a labour of love, with my own intention of doing something in the direction of creative writing.

You needn't remind me of the manuscript. I'll myself return it to you within a month. I believe in close reading.

I've just returned home from the press, having gone through the proofs of the special number on you of *Kakatiya Journal of English Studies*. So far 153 pages having been printed, the thing seems to go beyond 240 pages. Anyway, it will be a substantial number.

As for my own article on your idea of fiction, I have just started writing it. It will be a few weeks before the essay is completed. My apprehensions expressed in the earlier letters to you may be correct—the comprehensive article may have to appear in some other journal.

With affectionate regards,

Sincerely yours,
D. Ramakrishna

* * * * *

Bombay
April 15, 1977

Dear friend,

I have been in the North and was badly shaken by the earthquake. Since then, I have been trying to rescue some of my hopes from the debris.

I am telling everyone who ask me for an explanation, to read *Hamlet*.

I am grateful for your kind promise to look through the book of lectures. As they are lectures and nothing more or less, I would like to keep the form of the lectures *qua* lectures free enough, but controlled to the extent to which Morgan Forster controlled his class lectures.

But please be quite ruthless and cut out repetitions, put question marks against all the ambiguities and ask such things which have to be explained to the neo-literates, so that I can put in the explanations in footnotes at the end of each chapter.

I am grateful for the patience shown by Dr. Singh and yourself in the preparation of the special issue, but I can assure you that this collection which is a very unusual compilation, will help greatly to restore the balance of criticism of my novels and stories.

I am just rushing off to the country and will write to you again on my return before I leave for Delhi to preside on the Iqbal seminar.

Regards,

Yours sincerely,
Mulk Raj Anand

* * * * *

Warangal
May 18, 1977

Dear Dr. Anand,

I've had your letter of April 15. I trust that the Iqbal seminar was interesting.

I write this letter to say that I would not be able to complete work on *A Novel Form in the Ocean of Story* by the end of May as promised earlier. Kindly bear with me till the 15th of the next month. I assure you there won't be any further delay. Much work needs to be done on almost every page of the manuscript. The prose is effective, nevertheless. Your usage of commas is fantastic. Many of them should be removed. Also there are interesting things like Ravana being supplied with two extra heads, making him a twelve-headed demon. The names of ancient sages like Yajnavalkya have been consistently misspelled. I think we should take greater care while presenting our own culture to the outside world.

So far 210 pages of the special issue have been printed. Yesterday also I had to struggle with Atma Ram Sharma's article. Dr. Sharma's English is simply horrible. Anyway, we have completed the thing. Printing of his article having been completed, two pages of Dr. Balarama Gupta's essay have so far been composed. I think today Gupta's piece will be completed. Then follow the notes and the reviews, your "Why I write?" constituting the grand finale of the special number. By the way, I have enjoyed reading your interesting piece entitled "How I Became a Writer" in the May 1977 issue of *Mirror*. It's very inspiring indeed.

As for my own promised article on your "Theory of Fiction," I have a word of apology to offer. By the time I started writing the thing after engaging you in correspondence for a couple of months, printing of most of the publication was completed. Under some pressure, I simply manufactured a brief article tentatively and called it "Anand's Idea of the Novel" developing a couple of important points. The article has been printed. I confess I could not do a thorough article; but I assure you that your "idea" has not been distorted. However, my original article on your "Theory of Fiction" is still being shaped. By the end of the next month I will complete the thing and send it to you. I assure you the comprehensive article will be really representative of your theory or "hunches," as you put it.

With warm regards,

Sincerely yours,
D. Ramakrishna

* * * * *

Bombay
May 26, 1977

My dear young friend,

I was away from Bombay when your note of 18th May arrived.

I apologise for the eye strain I may have caused you with my MSS. I had not wanted to send it to you. In fact, I had told you that it was in no state to be read by anyone before I had gone through the whole thing. Unfortunately, through my preoccupation with the revision of the fourth novel of my series *Seven Ages of Man*, I could not find time to do this book. The Panjab University Publication Bureau has been waiting for the text for a year and a half.

I do not mind your taking longer time to look through this. And you can be ruthless as you like. I will not take umbrage.

I have, of course, to add many asides to my argument. I have done some notes during the last year; those I will add when you have finished.

Meanwhile, I don't envy you having to be at it in the heat of June.

I am not being polite when I say that I would like your pencilled notes, questions and challenges, so that I can answer them and supply the need which exists for a tentative critique of the whole Indian tradition of the recital-turned novel.

With warm regards,

Yours sincerely,
Mulk Raj Anand

* * * * *

Warangal
June 25, 1977

Dear Dr. Anand,

This is just a note to tell you that on the basis of your letter of May 26 I am still holding your MSS on the Indian novel. It's perhaps better if I return it to you personally when you come over here for the function to release the special number on you.

Well in advance I take this opportunity to request you to spare one hour of your precious time for me. I would like to sit with you alone and look into myself as in a mirror. I have completed seven short stories and sketches for two novels with typical Telugu background. If you could bless me to go ahead, I will be happy.

Kindly go through my piece on your "idea of fiction" and offer your comments. The more critical you are of my writing, the happier I will be. In such cases the other man's criticism becomes one's originality. Your comments will help me prepare the longer article I had originally planned.

Finally, a word of apology. I had to tamper with the cover design made by Dolly Sahiar by putting "Mulk Raj Anand Special Number" in the middle of the cover. In print, centring makes all the difference.

With best regards,

Yours sincerely,
D. Ramakrishna

* * * * *

Bombay
July 1, 1977

My dear young friend,

I feel like Goethe that in the face of the human predicament in a tragic and broken time, no literature, neither poetry nor prose fiction, can be any more than "barbarous composition." They are consolations against adversity, remnants shored against the ruin. It is no use applying the standards which we apply to the epic of Homer or the *Ramayana* and the *Mahabharata*. The age of the Gods is over. We can only see things from an evolutionary point of view, as in Tolstoy—birth, growth, maturity, decay, with a compassion for the situation and within this sordid experience, we can dispossess ourselves of all preconceived ideas and have the awareness of experience at all levels through direct "sensation." I would interpret "sensation" in the meaning of Guru Nanak. And the essence of the word would be vibration and not memory image only. In that sense, we may be in a position to create, or rather recreate, a parallel life, by analogy as it were, "poetry by analogy" against the prose that's what Forster meant when he said "only connect."

When I revise my lectures on the novel, I shall put in such hunches beyond your grammatical corrections and deletions as well as revisions.

I am reassured to see that, consciously or unconsciously, you also create each day as I tend to do, as a new day, by writing something or the other. It is wonderful to be able to achieve all the creative work you have done and it is a good thing to be a fool and rush in rather than be a wise professor and remain inhibited.

With warm regards,

Yours sincerely,
Mulk Raj Anand

* * * * *

Bombay
August 11, 1977

My dear young friend,

I have received your letter of 7th August just before I go off for MARG research in Rajasthan for ten days.

I am engaged or rather absorbed by the onerous task of stabilising this organisation. Many of our conceptualist friends and colleagues have never thought how important to me has been the 30 years' adventure into the interior refulgence of the plastic and pictorial arts. In fact, I feel that unless my attitude to the experience of creative works in other media and words is understood, there will be always complete misconception about my labyrinthine situations where the self is making itself by breaking itself and remaking itself again and again. It is strange to me that our intelligentsia is so far removed from the sources of creative imagination in our tradition that by reciting the mantra of the Advaita, they forget the millions of experiences in the Elan Vital which have been in our country. I think Tagore grasped this thing when he invented new methods of education specially by introducing music, dance and the pictorial arts into Shantiniketan. Our universities however, are barking up the wrong pole, if I may use an English cliché. That may be the reason why you want to see me. And I hope I can fill you with enough ardour to help to break down the whole pattern of the conventional British style degree awarding education.

I will certainly find time to come home to you.

With warm regards,

Yours sincerely,
Mulk Raj Anand

* * * * *

Warangal
August 23, 1977

Dear Dr. Anand,

Thank you for your kind letter of August 11. Containing a significant statement on your artistic pursuits, that is one of the most thoughtful letters I got from you. I hope you have successfully completed your tour of Rajasthan. When you come over here, you will be visiting a place called "Ramappa," famous for Kakatiya art. We put it in the tentative programme sent to you.

I am grateful to you for telling me that you would come home to me. Kindly make a note of it in your diary. This is purely a personal favour to me. In the course of that sitting with you, I will speak out what has been engaging my attention for more than a decade.

I have been observing the reaction of many academics to your work. While some blindly admire you purely for academic purposes, some go to the other extreme of condemning you. Keeping such "Deans of Letters" (as you describe a Bombay-wallah) in mind I have made extensive comments on your MSS. on the Indian novel. We will discuss these things also when we meet during your visit to Warangal.

Sincerely yours,
D. Ramakrishna

* * * * *

Warangal
September 25, 1977

Dear Dr. Anand,

Even through I couldn't "tape" my conversation with you, I carefully recorded your words in my mind and transcribed them on to my diary. Certain things remaining within my mind vaguely and somewhat troubling me over the years had been brought by you to the surface. Somehow I left your room in the Guest House on the 10th of September with the feeling that my dialogue with you was "unfinished." I think it was the right feeling an aspiring writer should develop. There cannot be a sense of finality so soon. I will visit Bombay within the next few years for a more detailed discussion with you. In the meantime, I will get stories (I have so far written) typed and improve them as much as I can.

You might have found my comments on your MSS. on the Indian novel useful. As I said in one of my letters to you, I have made those comments deliberately, keeping in mind some of your bitterest critics.

With warm regards,

Sincerely yours,
D. Ramakrishna

* * * * *

Bombay
October 7, 1977

My dear young friend,

I have been in the midst of proofs, proofs and texts in celebration of Sawai Jai Singh and have not had a moment to ask myself the stage of my health. Unfortunately, the breakdown of communications between the feudalists of the countryside and the typewriting community of Bombay is distressing. But we have not returned to the non-machine age of Morarjibhai and will go so far into the villages that we will become rumours to each other.

I did look into the MSS of my lectures on the novel and your notes cursorily. I am grateful for the guidelines you have given, the various question marks and the challenges. I will get down to the MSS if I can go away for a week or so to my country place.

Meanwhile, I want to apologise again for the atrociously badly typed text I sent you. But you may remember it was your fault, you wanted it at all costs and then you had to suffer the consequences of your urgency about having it.

I am the gainer by that much revision. And I hope to benefit from both the textual and the critical comments when I sit down to revise it finally for the press.

Unfortunately, many of these friends and myself are talking from different wavelengths. I am speaking from my hunches about the world novel and they are often thinking only in terms of the *Ramayana*, the *Mahabharata* and Sri Aurobindo. I don't think the Indians can gainsay the contribution to literature of the

West, especially of the Russians, the French and the German, who have seldom been read in our country.

I will write to you again, but may I thank you for the time you gave to the reading of my hopelessly muddled and badly typed manuscript.

Regards,

Yours sincerely,
Mulk Raj Anand

P.S. Do complete your book of stories. And go ahead with your novel. Try and get into "here-now" inside you, the quick of Andhra.

* * * * *

Bombay
December 28, 1977

My dear young friend,

This is to wish you a good New Year of struggle and effort and the will to come through!

I was in Delhi when your letter of 17th was received here. I went for the Coomaraswamy seminar.

I would have come South instead, but there was nothing in my hand concrete enough by way of a plan for the model village and I did not want to go to Andhra with empty hands.

By sheer coincidence I came across a young architect, who has designed a foolproof house, which can withstand any storms and he has already built such houses in Haryana. He took me round and proved to me that this human habitation can be made for Rs. 4,000.

Since then, I got three offers to sponsor the model village and I am busy correlating various factors, specially the receiving end which is the A.P. Government, who will have to allot the land. I have written all round, sent telegrams minus anger, and hope that the careless hearts of the politicians will melt. I have written to the woman Governor or Governess to persuade her charges into collaboration.

If the A.P. Government melts, even to the extent of giving land for one village, I will come South in this connection.

But it is important to have someone like you for a week or so travelling with us, both to interpret and to give us the directions. Do you think you can take a week or ten days' leave—somewhere around the last week of January? It is not quite certain, so please don't finalise.

Meanwhile, I at least find that in the face of a deluge of the dimension of the cyclone in Andhra, I can't write from any detachment. And the politicking in Delhi and elsewhere fills me with disgust, almost existentialist despair.

I hope things mature and we will meet.

With warm regards,

Yours sincerely,
Mulk Raj Anand

* * * * *

Warangal
January 3, 1978

Dear Dr. Anand,

Thank you very much for your letter of December 28 blessing me on the eve of the New Year. I wish you too a very fruitful New Year.

I've shown your letter to several of my friends here. We all sincerely thank you for the deep sympathy that you have evinced for the suffering humanity in Andhra. At a time when the Indian literary scene is filled with writers and pseudo-writers who are either devoid of conviction or simply lost in fantasies unconnected with the actualities of life, yours is the sole voice heard across the subcontinent for a practical application of the human principle that is the real objective of the creative writer. Whatever the politicking going on in New Delhi and Hyderabad, I have no doubt that the A.P. Government will invite you to the State to construct the model village.

What I hear from my people in the cyclone-hit area is that the amount of Rs. 150/- given to each family is not reaching the needy. Only a part of the amount is being given to the person concerned and his signature or thumb impression is taken for the whole! There has been widespread official and non-official corruption—a part of the Indian scene. Prisoners released from the

State Prison to burn the dead bodies and carcasses have collected jewellery and other valuables and promptly submitted them to the officials. But the others—official and non-official—in charge of the rescue operations are known to have simply swindled such properties on large scale. Thus you and your team should ensure that the moneys you are spending, the houses you are constructing, do not become the property of middlemen and profiteers. Only then your humanitarian efforts would be meaningful, reaching the grateful souls for whom they are intended.

Best regards,

Yours sincerely,
D. Ramakrishna

* * * * *

Bombay
February 10, 1978

My dear young friend,

I have come back from my research tour of Karnataka and Tamilnadu full of the euphoria of the beauties, splendours and glories I have seen in the ancient monuments.

Unfortunately, I was not able to do any more than motor upto the coastline of lower A.P. to see the cyclone-affected area. And my visit to Guntur and Machilipatnam has had to be postponed in view of the fact that the A.P. Government is now involved in elections. With the fever having spread everywhere, I thought this plague may be allowed to work itself out and I would then go a little pure at heart, to the Guntur area.

I am grateful for the cordial letter you have sent me giving me the information about whom to approach in the Government.

Actually, I wrote to the Governor of A.P. and she has responded very sympathetically to the idea of the projected model village.

I am trying to get more concrete advice from her.

But I have to go to Delhi today to Chair a session of the Triennial seminar and will be able to make my plans for coming to A.P. on my return.

Meanwhile, the Principal of Ravi's College, Guntur, has kindly invited me and offered to make arrangements for transport.

This may make it possible for me to come to Hyderabad by the middle of March after attending the Coomaraswamy seminar in Mysore University and then go by road to Guntur and Machilipatnam.

I will write to you before I go to Mysore and perhaps you can join me in Hyderabad for a two or three day trip to the coastal area.

Please forgive this dusty letter, but I am just preparing to leave by the afternoon plane for Delhi.

Regards,

Yours sincerely,
Mulk Raj Anand

* * * * *

Bombay
March, 22, 1978

My dear young friend,

Mea Culpa!

But the circumstances of my visit to the cyclone-affected area were very peculiar.

I had fever of 102^0 when I went to Mysore for the Coomaraswamy seminar. I had temperature every day during the seminar and I did not think it would be possible to venture out to Guntur at all. Luckily the antibiotics helped and against docotor's advice, I decided to keep my date with Mr. Dhan. There was no time at that juncture to write to you. At any rate, in Bangalore, I did not know that the A.P. Government would be cordial. On reaching Hyderabad, I found that Smt. Sharada Mukherjee had laid on the arrangements for my visit to the cyclone area. And Mr. Dhan had gone to the extent of providing a vehicle which I had not anticipated. I did not want to entail any expenses to you during my visit, even in the situation where a private person was helping me and Mr. Dhan never told me that he was asking you.

As it turned out, Mr. Dhan went out of his way to spend a fair amount of money on my visit.

And after the lecture the next day, the Government gave me a car from Vijayawada.

The visit was successful, because the land for the village was indicated to me and the indigent families are on the list of the Collector and the whole operation can take place.

But I have to mount a campaign to collect one and half lakh of rupees from the intelligentsia.

Unfortunately, apart from you, no one offered to come with me, except an artist from Guntur.

Therefore, it was not because I wanted to spurn the offer you made. I wanted to involve you at a stage when apart from tea and sympathy, we can make a committee to raise money first in Andhra and then elsewhere.

I have begun by asking the Kalamkari workers to donate Kalamkaris for an auction and they have agreed. Is it possible to ask the Kakatiya University people to raise five or ten thousand? Then with the money I raise we will go there, with some integrity.

Regards,

Yours sincerely,
Mulk Raj Anand

* * * * *

Bombay
April 14, 1978

Dear Friend,

I have just returned from the Spring festival we organised for our offering—*In Praise of Hoyasala Art*, in Bangalore. I brought the Spring air with me, though the perfume is dissolving in the sweat of Maharashtra.

I am finding the conscience of the intellectuals congealed behind the dread of feeling pity for the poor. But there are a few people who will, I know, awaken. I was moved by the fact that the Kalamkari craftsmen offered to help immediately as I appealed to them. So if we don't get much response from the tolerably well-off, I don't mind starting a rupee fund from the poor.

I will report to you the progress as we go along.

Regards,

Yours sincerely,
Mulk Raj Anand

* * * * *

Bombay
April 19, 1978

My dear friend,

I have been away in Bangalore for the inauguration of the MARG offering *In Praise of Hoyasala Art*. We organised a kind of Spring festival. And we were able to involve a good many literati and scientists in the visual and the plastic situations about which the Indian intelligentsia has said nothing very much. On my return home, I saw your letter of April 12, and confirm for myself that I have read your article on Poets and Poetasters. I had felt then I should write to compliment you and ask you to do a critique of this kind every now and then. It seems to me you have got the essence of the situation about the critics. Those like Jussawalla are hovering over an existentialist area. Meenakshi Mukherjee turns Durga, Parvati and Kali in turn and assumes those incarnations. Shahane is insensitive and dotes on Khushwant Singh. And P. Lal judges everything from the heights of the Advaita. Meanwhile, the categories cannot conform to the miscellaneousness of reality and the total view is lost. It is inevitable, in the fragmented time, with fragmented minds, dealing with fragmented bits and pieces of our society, without an ethos. Time will tell. Meanwhile, I hope you can get hold of *So Many Freedoms*, by Dr. Cowasjee, and review it somewhere. A book from Dr. Niven will follow from Arnold-Heinemann next month.

The total response to my appeal for funds in BLITZ for the Kalamkari village was Re.1.25. I paid the postman a tip of Rs.1/- but I have generous response from foreigners and am busy organising an auction of art works.

I will report to you what happens as we go along. I am not giving up.

Regards,

Yours sincerely,

Mulk Raj Anand

* * * * *

Warangal
April 22, 1978

Dear Dr. Anand,

Thank you very much for your kind letter saying some good things about my article on Poets and Poetasters. Not only as teacher and researcher but as editor at the American Studies Research Centre in Hyderabad for four years I have had an opportunity to probe into the minds of the Indian (Academic) critics. I just wanted to say what I have so intensely felt about the corrupt state of criticism in India. Normally, academics take sides with this or that writer and indiscriminately and thoughtlessly condemn others that do not belong to their clique. At times I cannot help wondering whether these "criticasters" are morally superior to the semiliterate politicians lost in petty skirmishes, of course, ultimately leading to earthquakes of the Delhi dimensions.

It's sad that the response for your project in Andhra is so slow. Nevertheless, I have no doubt that ultimately people will show greater enthusiasm. At least five academics in the various universities and colleges have written to me that they would send some money to you.

Best Regards,

Sincerely,
D. Ramakrishna

* * * * *

Bombay
May 3, 1978

My dear friend,

As the warm weather hots up and the political situation becomes hotter, the intellectual situation becomes a little fuzzy.

I am pondering over the reasons why there is such inertia in university circles. My own Panjab University is far worse than any other.

But I am persisting in my campaign on another level. I am doing a whole book on Kalamkaris, arranging exhibitions of the wonderful work in three or four places and hoping to raise money, at least some part, from the contributions which the Kalamkari workers have offered by way of 50 pieces which will be auctioned. I know the poor are very generous, so I would like to make their contribution the first and the initial one.

About your intention to write on the works of Nayantara Sahgal, I think it is a good idea, but please do not do a comparison of my fiction with hers. Already she thinks that I am against her, because I have not considered any of her books yet, worthy of a Sahitya Akademi award. After her early fiction, she had begun to make cardboard characters. And deals with a pseudo-elite whom I know only too well to be effete poseurs, brown sahibs and memsahibs of the India International Centre, with ambitions poised in Fifth Avenue.

As she is younger than me by many years, I would not like her to feel that old uncle Mulk has not yet been got out of the way, and is a damned nuisance, standing between youth and age.

Why not compare her to Kamala Markandaya, who, though also elitist, on the basis of her lower middle class affiliations in England, comes through as a more sincere writer at least in the early books.

Please do not think that I am being vicious. I only want to avoid the ganging up of Khushwant Singh, Dom Moraes and Nayantara Sahgal in Delhi with a gossip campaign about my being a bloody red, exciting Naxalites to put bombs underneath the chair of Morarji Desai.

I hope you will get the book on Cowasjee from O.U.P. But I am afraid they may refuse it, unless *Kakatiya Journal* asks for it. Or you could ask Literary Editor, *Deccan Herald*, if you can review it for them. You can write to the Literary Editor and mention that I have encouraged you to ask for the book, if it has not been given away to somebody else.

Regards,

Yours sincerely,
Mulk Raj Anand

* * * * *

Warangal
July 11, 1978

Dear Dr. Anand,

You wrote to me a postcard hurriedly before leaving for Khandala to escape from the heat of the summer, saying you would write a more elaborate letter afterwards. By this time you might have resettled in Bombay for active work. You do not seem to have had any response for the model village. It's a pity man in the modern India is so indifferent not only to his fellow men but ultimately to himself. Is it the Indian's great inheritance of the Karmic philosophy? This philosophical resignation bordering upon callousness is both the blessing and the bane of the Indian mind.

It's heartening to note that the mid-summer madness in New Delhi's political circles has been somewhat cured by the onset of the monsoon. In the midst of such a din Mrs. Nayantara Sahgal continues to shout for an intellectual revolt. Yesterday again she wrote an article entitled "Stuck in the Status Quo" in *The Indian Express*. I have written to her about it and her recent novel *A Situation in New Delhi*. She talks so much about "revolution," "change," and all that, but ultimately comes out with no positive solutions. This happens in *A Situation in New Delhi* also. All that stands for revolution, coming down from Jawaharlal Nehru, ends in the fate of Usman, Devi and Rishad. Nayantara ultimately returns to the cosy nook of aristocracy in New Delhi's socialistic politics.

A few weeks ago Raj Kumari Indira Devi Dhanrajgiri and her husband Sri Seshendra Sarma were here and I had an opportunity to talk to them for several hours. Mrs. Indira Devi told me that you had been at their Gyan Bagh Palace last year. They are doing good service to Telugu literature. While Seshendra is a brilliant critic and modern Telugu poet, Mrs. Indira Devi is trying to do something in the direction of Indo-English poetry.

What have you done with your manuscript on the Indian novel? I think you should give it to the press at the earliest. It will be a landmark in the criticism of Indian novel. Why don't you offer it to some publisher in U.K. or U.S.A.?

With warm regards,

Sincerely yours,

D. Ramakrishna

* * * * *

Bombay
July 19, 1978

Dear Ramakrishna,

The escape from the heat of summer turned out to be a bout of malaria. Since then there have been feverish activities trying to organise a monograph on Kalamkaris, along with an exhibition of the most important places which has been promised by the All-India Handicrafts Board, to take place in Bombay, Hyderabad, Guntur, Bangalore and Madras. We may be able to raise money for the Kalamkari Village that way by a few auctions.

I got three houses so far starting off with an offer from myself of Rs. 5,000 from the advance on the textbook edition of *Untouchable*, adopted by the Mysore University for three years. The other two have come from abroad. But somehow or the other, I fulfill my promise to myself and the Kalamkari workers of Machilipatnam.

This has left me little time for the writing work, though I am busy revising *The Bubble*. I find that the absence of a congenial atmosphere, like that of London or Paris where creative work is taken seriously, makes the writing a lonely affair, but still there is enough discreet pleasure in remembrances of things past, to make life worthwhile, so long as one is at it. And in the new novel I am daring to make technical innovations, following closely upon my first draft of the 20s when I had the presumption that I had anticipated Andre Gide in his novel *Counterfeiters*. Actually it was so, that on my own I had begun to believe in 25, 26, 27 that anything could make a novel, because Prof. Dobree said so; forthwith I had knit together letters, diaries, journals, and a novel within them all through the sheer attempt to be clever as one tries to do when one is young. And though I found confirmation in Paris that I had been doing something parallel to Gide's novel, I did not know French and, therefore, got to know that Gide had done it in a masterly manner, while I was a novice. Since then, however, I have had the benefit of reading Gide, so that I can be like him and yet different.

The trouble with our younger friends is that most of them come from the English-speaking middle class milieu. And they believe that giving up chocolate cake and going to jail for a month makes them into revolutionists. Therefore, they can't even get as far as uncle Nehru. Only Tara has shown some courage in leaving her businessman husband and living with an ex-ICS official. All the same she is stuck in the status quo. She would have to move out of Delhi to her native Uttar Pradesh to be with the Bhayas before she can talk of revolution. I learnt that truth when I left her mother's house in Lucknow to go and live in Kalakankar and wrote *The Sword and the Sickle*.

There have been one or two smash-ups of *So Many Freedoms*. More on the way. But Cowasjee is incurable and will only realise how far unjust he is when he reads Dr. Niven's book in a month or two from Arnold-Heinemann.

I am hoping to get at the "Novel Form in the Ocean of Story," when I can swim out from the bubbles. May come to Hyderabad for the Forster seminar in January. Then a visit to Warangal, though probably you may also come to Hyderabad then. Before that, when I revise the novel form, I want you to have another look at the MSS.

Regards,

Yours sincerely,
Mulk Raj Anand

* * * * *

Bombay
September 22, 1978

Dear friend,

I have been meaning to write to you for some days.

Quite recently, my publisher Gulab Vazirani and I were in Pune together and had occasion to meet Prof. Raina of the English Department of Pune University.

It seems the Board of Studies of this University is looking for an anthology of Indian English prose.

Mr. Vazirani wondered who could do this anthology and I mentioned your name as a most likely person who could do the work from perceptive understanding of the whole pioneer tradition of the modern-contemporary period.

Of course, both Dr. Raina and myself have some views on this theme and could help you if you do not consider such an offer impertinent.

As you know, an emergent style like Indian-English needs collaboration between at least two people to check and counter-check the selections.

If you feel that you would do this work in consultation with myself and Dr. Raina, I could ask Arnold-Heinemann to commission the work to you.

Do write quickly as I am likely to go to Kerala for the Vallathol Seminar and then to Canada for the Commonwealth Writers Conference.

With warm regards,

Yours sincerely,
Mulk Raj Anand

* * * * *

Bombay
October 10, 1978

Dear Ramakrishna,

This morning suddenly Mr. Shahane rang up from Delhi to ask if he could see me tomorrow. I have asked him to lunch. It seems Gulab Vazirani may have suggested to him to dissolve his antagonism to me and he may have been reminded that after all, I am the oldest writer whose name will ever remain linked up with Forster for his friendship for the once rejected me and his friendship to *Untouchable*, apart from the E.M. Forster Award given to me for *Confession of a Lover*. There is such a thing as objectivity. And the Indian-English writers might realise that without his powerful support to the first three musketeers, Indian-English fiction may not have been recognised as quickly as it was in the Thirties. And perhaps we could take from Forster the values of generosity, friendship and grace, which he owed in some part to his intimate relations with cultured Indians.

Anyhow, I suppose I shall eventually be asked by the reluctant Dr. Shahane to the seminar.

I go to Canada on the 16th returning on the 31st.

Regards,

Yours sincerely,
Mulk Raj Anand

* * * * *

Bombay
November 17, 1978

My dear friend,

I returned from the Commonwealth Writers Conference and plunged right into the Festival of Arts we organised for Shri Dinkar Kelkar, an old man who has assembled one of the finest museums of the folk art in the world during the last 50 years in Pune. This was a roaring success—literally because over thirty thousand people participated in it. So MARG is going deeper into interior consciousness.

I find that in the outside world, the young are more responsive to new values and sidetrack traditionalism. I got a very warm reception in the seven universities I visited.

With warm regards,

Yours sincerely,
Mulk Raj Anand

* * * * *

Bombay
March 6, 1979

Dear Friend,

On my return from Delhi I have seen your letter of February 1, 1979, and the postcard of February 23.

During my visit to Arnold-Heinemann office, Mr. Vazirani showed me the list of contents of your Anthology of Indian English prose.

I am impressed by the amount of labour which you have put into this work and I am sure it will be a pioneer book which will help many students and interested parties to see the making of a new language which will, I am sure, ultimately come to be recognised both in our country and abroad as a vital culture.

From the comprehensive list and number of pages mentioned, there seems to be a danger of the anthology becoming longer than might be feasible under present conditions of publishing. Have you reckoned up the number of pages it will make?

Mr. Vazirani and I felt that a book of about 300 pages altogether would be a fair proposition. Or may be 250 pages. In either case the price will have to be kept down, so that later a text-book edition can become possible and accessible to students at a modest price.

Or do you think you could cut down the insertions or choose different ones in case of those authors where the extract is too long?

Please do not think that I do not appreciate the labour and the hard work you have put in.

And, if necessary, you can ignore the dateline.

I am sending a copy of this letter to Dr. Raina and asking him for his own comments.

Regards,

Yours sincerely,
Mulk Raj Anand

P.S.: I will be in Hyderabad from 22nd March till about 7th April for the Kalamkari festival.

* * * * *

Bombay
April 6, 1979

Dear Ramakrishna,

This is to apologise to you for the inconvenience caused. Everyone was sent a telegram about the postponement of the exhibition/festival Homage to Kalamkari, as from MARG, but my personal friends were not on the list. Sorry. But the precarious condition of Jayaprakash Narain made it difficult to have festivities when this good man was lying between life and death. And we did not wish to behave like Morarji Desai. I hope you will understand this last minute cancellation and forgive the trouble caused to you.

I am afraid I cannot get any response from Prof. Raina to any letters or postcards. There is a blind spot somewhere in his mind and for years I have not been able to fathom what is behind it.

I do not agree with Shiv Kumar about the title. Certainly Indo-Anglian is horrible. Anyhow this is not an important question yet.

I will let you have suggestion about the quotation for my writings later after brooding a little while.

I am reassured that Mr. Vazirani has taken my advice in spite of his well-known proclivities to close his fist as soon as an author asks for money. Do go ahead and utilise the time of the vacations to finish this work.

I hope to settle the new date for the exhibition possibly to begin after the rains have started. We were told by friends from Hyderabad that April is a cruel month. And I hope not to mislead you again.

Regards,

Yours sincerely,
Mulk Raj Anand

* * * * *

Bombay
May 15, 1979

Dear Ramakrishna,

As for Bhabani Bhattacharya—he has always been an imitationalist, first of Hemingway, Bull OX style. Then he followed other American models. Perhaps an extract from his book on the influence of Gandhiji on Indian literature may be found good enough, to bring out the aura of influence exercised by the Mahatma on us all.

Yours sincerely,
Mulk Raj Anand

* * * * *

Bombay
May 30, 1979

Dear Ramakrishna,

I understand that Mr. Vazirani has gone off to U.K. and U.S.A. on his bi-annual tour. I see that his firm does not mind spending several thousand rupees on his airfares and hotels, but doesn't permit him to pay the copyright fee as demanded by the publishers.

One of them should ask him what he would do if he was asked for copyright fee for a book by some other publisher or an anthology.

Anyhow, you try and secure as much as you can, more or less free of copyright, and for the rest, Arnold-Heinemann should pay or negotiate.

I can only tell him this when he returns.

In case he refuses, I will pay the Rs. 500/- back on your behalf, which was advanced to you and I can place the book for you with a publisher who will pay you properly to defray all your expenses and my loan as well.

Incidentally, I noticed a very fine passage in Chagla's book *Roses for December*. It is towards the end of his biography. I will give you the proper contacts next week.

Regards,

Yours sincerely,
Mulk Raj Anand

* * * * *

Bombay
June 6, 1979

Dear friend,

Your note of 21st May.

It may be a good idea to get as many quotations from books and authors as possible, without payment, but there is no reason why Vazirani should not pay for such extracts as are not available without copyright fee.

On principle, I think it is very unfair of Vazirani when he is publishing a book which might be commercially viable, not to want to pay the copyright fee.

In case he doesn't want to fulfil this obligation, I will pay him the advance he has given you and get you another publisher.

As you can imagine, it is very invidious for me as a co-drafter of the Authors Guild contract form, to ignore copyright conventions. So I will not write to National Book Trust and Publications Division; only when you write, remind them again. You can mention that I instigated this book and as it is educational could they charge only a nominal fee.

About a quotation from me, I think the choice could be between Lakha's story told almost in literal translation from Punjabi and "Eagles and Pigeons," the last short story in *Barber's Trade Union* and "A Village Idyll," a love story of a village boy and girl.

If the anthology is very heavy you might consider giving your students at least three or four short stories or fables rather than merely conditioned or didactic prose. The average student I find is unable to swallow more than a mouthful of the rhetoric of our politicians old and new. Though in the case of Rajaji why not give one of his fables either original or in translation of one of the stories in the Upanishad.

I should do the same with all the creative writers.

I suppose you know that Bankim Chander wrote his very first novel in English. I think it is called *Rajmohan's Wife*.

And while you sweat away in the heat of Andhra Pradesh, you might consider relaxing a little from your labours to wait patiently for Mr. Vazirani who has gone off to enjoy the English summer and the American swelter for a month, to the tune of nearly Rs. 50000 in expenses.

Regards

Yours sincerely,
Mulk Raj Anand

* * * * *

Bombay
August 7, 1979

Dear Ramakrishna,

After the Kalamkari festival, even before it finished, I went away to Karnataka and Kerala to arrange two more festivals for our book on Aihole and Kerala Heritage.

All the intelligentsia of Andhra Pradesh was asked to the Kalamkari exhibition and performing arts programme. But except for Shiv Kumar and Raina, no one came. I think the Professors are dead at heart. They only know how to repeat the words of other people and have little sense of wonder in their eye.

I wondered why my letter didn't get to you, but now I see what happened.

I have seen Vazirani's letter asking for the revised list from you. So perhaps you may go on with him, since this may be his indirect way of admitting he was wrong asking for the list.

I think you might persist and get the copyrights at the lowest rates. And then the formula I suggested that Arnold-Heinemann might offer you a lesser royalty and pay for the copyrights from a percentage. Maybe considered fair by both parties. Prof. Raina was very hopeful about possibilities in Pune for this book and he seems to like your work. He spent an evening with us in Hyderabad.

In case Mr. Vazirani goes along with the anthology, you can just tear my cheque up and let me know, that you have done so.

With warm regards,

Yours sincerely,
Mulk Raj Anand

* * * * *

Bombay
August 30, 1979

Dear Ramakrishna,

Your letter of August 22nd found me involved in the troubles of Dr. Raina. It seems he has been accused of smiling at the girls and giving them more marks than to the boys. An inquiry committee headed by the Vice-Chancellor of old times, cleared him. But some malicious people are still carrying on a vicious campaign against him and he is in a state of breakdown. Therefore, please don't expect any letter from him, to tell you how good your book is. You take it from me that the conscientious job you have done cannot fail to be worthy of your scholarship and you must have the confidence to go ahead on your own steam. But go right ahead and if Mr. Vazirani has not said 'no', he will do it.

As you probably don't know, Mr. Roly-Poly is going to Moscow next week, coming back for ten days and going to

Frankfurt. That is the way he does his publishing. Since the English woman Editor he had last year, he has no Editor. But he has the confidence of the lord and won't be told anything. Any-how, so long as he gets the book as cheap as he is getting, he will be all right. You must remember it's in-built thing in the Sindhis.

I did a long tour by motor from Bangalore, Trivandrum and back, and that has not improved my spondylitis, but still I carry on in spite of the doctor's advice not to strain myself.

Regards,

Yours sincerely,
Mulk Raj Anand

* * * * *

Bombay
September 28, 1979

Dear friend,

It is reassuring that Mr. Roly-Poly has written to you. He will soon be on the way to Frankfurt and then to London for a day or so, when he will be too busy lunching at the Savoy to work for you or I. His Principals seem to regard him as a colonial stooge. So do not put too many hopes in the anthology being accepted in London.

I will be happy enough to see it prosper in India and Africa.

I have seen your reviews—they were thoughtful, though Prof. Shiv Kumar's novel is not important and too biased against women. Strange—I had not thought him capable of such anger. Please don't tell him this, I will tell myself one day.

And I should have finished your anthology before you go on to the other works.

Regards,

Yours sincerely,
Mulk Raj Anand

* * * * *

Bombay
November 22, 1979

Dear Ramakrishna,

I have your note of 17th November and feel that you are well on the job now and everything goes well.

Only as the International Book Fair starts on 1st March next year, it would be a good thing if the book could come out by that time. So please write to Mr. Vazirani to get the copyrights for those items which he can get.

As for Nirad Chaudhuri, again ask Mr. Vazirani if he can intervene.

So conscientious a scholar as you deserves all the success possible and it will surely come to you.

I don't know what is your anger on Poe, but he was an exile to life and tormented by lack of spiritual growth and therefore became neurotic using his illness to produce the tales of horror and imagination. A typical product of the sensitive individual's reaction against the hardness of America.

Please keep me informed of developments.

Regards,

Yours sincerely,
Mulk Raj Anand

* * * * *

Bombay
January 30, 1980

Dear Ramakrishna,

I have returned from Madras after a very happy sojourn during which our volume on Bharata Natyam was inaugurated by Smt. Rukmini Devi and I am full of the euphoria of the seven days' recital I saw.

What a great art is Bharata Natyam and yet how few of the literary intelligentsia know anything about it. I hope your book reaches Delhi when I am there after the middle of this month.

Regards,

Yours sincerely,
Mulk Raj Anand

* * * * *

Bombay
May 21, 1980

Dear Ramakrishna,

I have been abroad for a seminar, that is why you have not heard from me.

I am reassured that you have sent the book to Mr. Vazirani and the proofs are already on the way. And it is further reassuring that this publisher, a hard taskmaster, has at last appreciated your efforts in this compilation and your integrity. It seems to me, in general, that through the lack of faith in Indian English writing, both of the university people and the publishers, there is hardly any evidence of its emergence in countries abroad, not that there is much sign of our books in the commercial bookshops. Arthur Hailey, Mario Pugo, Alistair MacLean, James Hadley Chase and Jacqueline Susane are everywhere in airports, on the pavements and on the railway bookstalls. It is the same in mid-Asia. The American commercialists have dumped all markets.

And here we all want to get back to Shankara one way or another, so that repeating Shivom will make us nobler. The destination man of Jawaharlal which promised uplift through an overall spirituality inspired by emergence of the will to happiness has been forgotten in the quest for personal gain and there we are talking of spirituality in terms of Sai Baba.

I hope your anthology will help to show the confusion.

With warm regards,

Yours sincerely,
Mulk Raj Anand

* * * * *

Bombay
June 10, 1980

Dear young friend,

I returned from abroad a fortnight ago sooner than Mr. Vazirani thought. I had only gone for a seminar to Amman, Jordan, and nowadays I find travelling anywhere certainly to foreign countries, like going through an Indian hell, Arab purgatory and a European nightmare.

I am reassured that things have gone well for you and it is surprising that Mr. Vazirani woke up to the importance of your book after all. Maybe, since giving up the Presidentship of the Publishers Association, he has a little more time for publishing.

I am finalising the typescript of *The Bubble*, but the lack of good typists in our country growingly makes it difficult to get even one page of presentable typescript to a publisher abroad.

If you have finished your book by the end of June, and have time, I would like you to go through the new novel.

Regards,

Yours sincerely,
Mulk Raj Anand

* * * * *

June 25, 1980

Dear Ramakrishna,

I did not sense that Poe had much craft to him, though he had a fervid imagination. In fact, I feel that in his case, the fantasy dictated reverberations beyond the technique of the usual short story or novel. In fact, in some ways he is the precursor of James Joyce in his love of sound vibrations and imaginative extension of feeling into terror and horror.

Anyhow, please forgive my amateurish remarks, because I am not a professional critic.

Regards,

Yours sincerely,
Mulk Raj Anand

* * * * *

Bombay
July 3, 1980

Dear Ramakrishna,

Your note of 30th June.

You know I would rather expect people read my books than that they gave me more honorary degrees. With three or four of these already, I begin to feel like a donkey, carrying a big load of honorary learning.

When I was a young struggling writer in Bloomsbury, with friends like Louis Macniece, Dylan Thomas, and Philip Henderson, eating steak and kidney pie, with tea in my attic studio in Woburn Buildings, we used to laugh at the number of students who would get doctor's degree for writing theses about the poems and novels we were writing, and we used to be amused when Oxford or Cambridge had a convocation which conferred honorary degrees on men like W.B. Yeats. The more degrees he got, the less we wanted to read him. I am afraid, this is going to be the fate of people like myself. Already I can see the younger generation putting the old uncles on the shelf. Mrs. Shyamala Narayan says, I am, with Ahmed Abbas, a social realist, whatever that may mean.

Mrs. Meenakshi Mukherjee says, I am a fake; and Dom Moraes says I am in his way because I write too much. And so it goes on. The overthrowing of the old uncles into the limbo.

Anyhow, people like myself feel that we can't survive without creativeness. I see that people like Charles Snow who stopped writing, just lapsed physically also.

With warm regards,

Yours sincerely,
Mulk Raj Anand

* * * * *

Bombay
November 21, 1980

My dear friend Ramakrishna,

Greetings!

I returned from Cambridge after delivering my lectures about ten days ago rather tired from the air journey and much dispirited by the breakdown of values in the West. I am afraid, the northerners are completely oblivious of the southerners and have become a kind of hell people as the Jains may call them each one more neurotic than the other.

Personally I was able to fulfil my nostalgia by the return to Cambridge, the green grass, the weeping willows shedding their tears into the river Cam. I found the intelligentsia warm and affectionate and the new young were willing to listen, specially the Africans, the West Indians and the new generation of Indians born in U.K. from émigré parents. I was reassured to find that they all went to inherit *Untouchable* and go on towards their own expressionism from the prototype I offered in my protest novel.

This was reassuring because unlike many of the Indian intellectuals and creative writers, the new young elsewhere have gone on beyond the literature of pure pleasure and salvationism to the literature of confrontation of realities.

I was happy to hear that your book has met with a warm response. I am sure if Mr. Vazirani can place his big bottom on a chair long enough to attend to his publications, your book will go very far. Unfortunately, he was on pleasure bent and went round the world with his wife and daughter for the third time in five years.

Actually, my lectures in Cambridge were based on the book about the MS which you read. I took the opportunity of the leisurely mornings to revise the text, benefiting here and there from your comments and I hope to fill in some footnotes and ask the Panjab University to allow it to be published internationally.

I was able to place a book of *Conversations in Bloomsbury* in U.K. almost immediately on arrival. And the interview published by the *Guardian* as well as the BBC made me somewhat of a monument, which means one can be a prophet abroad and not in one's own country.

Do let me see photostat copies of the reviews of your book.

Regards,

Yours sincerely,
Mulk Raj Anand

* * * * *

Bombay
July 22, 1981

Dear Ramakrishna,

As you have rightly guessed, I have been busy with the invigilation Committee for T.V. and A.I.R. And there has been a crisis here which has led me to resign from *Marg* in protest against the favouritism of *Marg* Chairman, Mr. Bhabha, who brought into disgrace the liberal tradition of his brother, the late Homi Bhabha. I shall tell you more about it one day. Meanwhile, there is nothing to mourn in the breakdown of my connection with this publishing house, which I founded. I already have various offers and the worthwhile books which I had planned will come out, five a year from a big publisher in Bombay. Also, I shall be released for National Work, as I have been appointed

Chairman of the Cultural Committee for ASIAD '82 and am also Adviser in the National Book Trust. I shall now have time to finish my novel, the remaining three volumes. *The Bubble* goes to press next month.

I was reassured to read the reviews of your book *Indian English Prose*. I think by and large, they are commendatory and may have been some compensation for your arduous work on the compilation under difficult conditions.

Of course, there is a crisis in the book industry and Mr. Vazirani tells me that U.G.C. has still not given any grant for the last two years for the libraries to purchase books. I am afraid, like other things in the country, there is no straightforward going on in any department of human affairs and the crisis is going to become much deeper, probably squeezing out culture, education and health, because of the defence preparations India has to make. Perhaps the intelligentsia will wake up from its isolation and think of ways by which they can participate in renovating the education system and create new consciousness.

I am going for a research tour to Ladakh next month after my Doordarshan meetings in Delhi and hope that I might come to Hyderabad later in the year.

With warm regards,

Yours sincerely,
Mulk Raj Anand

* * * * *

Bombay
March 3, 1982

Dear friend Ramakrishna,

I am always happy to hear from you, at this stage of my life, perhaps always I am not interested in awards or rewards but in doing my duty to the Arts from love of duty and tenderness. I go to Delhi again this evening and I am forced to be brief.

Yours sincerely,
Mulk Raj Anand

* * * * *

Warangal
June 2, 1982

Dear Dr. Anand,

I wrote to you on the 24th of May, I'm happy to know from this morning newspaper that you have been appointed Honorary Editor of the art books to be published by the GOI's Publications Division. The centre of your activity seems to have shifted to the country's capital. Instead of the Tatas gaining from your skills in art, the government and the people of the country will hereafter greatly benefit. I look forward to seeing impressive art publications under your distinguished editorship.

Yours sincerely,
D. Ramakrishna

* * * * *

Bombay
June, 23, 1982

Dear Ramakrishna,

Your good wishes and your postcard of 2nd June arrived here in my absence. And now I go to London tomorrow for the Indian-English seminar in the Commonwealth Institute where R.K. Narayan, Raja Rao and Anita Desai are also coming.

As there is nothing much in common with the Commonwealth except the English language, I go in a rather cynical mood, though I must confess that the English are far more generous to Indian-English than the Indians.

Maybe we shall meet in the autumn.

Regards,

Yours sincerely,
Mulk Raj Anand

* * * * *

Bombay
August 10, 1982

Dear Ramakrishna,

I had been in U.K. for the Indian-English literature seminar. Then I was in France for some research in the Museum of Man and to see Lascaux cave paintings of 20000 years ago—miraculous!

I found there is much attention being paid to Indian-English Writings abroad. In our own country the critics tear up everything written by those who don't belong to their own gang. It is sad, but true, that every Indian intellectual denigrates the other. In view of this, I am reassured, that you are receiving attention.

With warm regards,

Yours sincerely,
Mulk Raj Anand

* * * * *

Bombay
August 28, 1982

Dear Dr. Ramakrishna,

There was much more cordial response to the papers with humanistic reference than to the perverse Nirad Chaudhuri speech or to the exalted utterances in the London Seminar. And Mrs. Mukherjee wanted someone to take up research in the 30s movement. So, good sense will prevail.

This is a brief note, because I go to a UNESCO conference in Istanbul at the end week. And on my return I shall be preparing to go to Brisbane for another Commonwealth Literary Seminar.

Regards,

Yours sincerely,
Mulk Raj Anand

* * * * *

Bombay
December 22, 1982

Dear Ramakrishna,

I have been in the Punjab of late, mourning the loss of all the values of the freedom struggle. And when, on my return, I read your letter, I felt how removed is our intelligentsia, including yourself, from the problems of our non-emergent contemporary Indian civilization.

I can understand Nissim Ezekiel's censure of the social dynamics seminar in Hyderabad. But I can't understand that the themes you are encouraging your students to take up have little relevance to our predicament.

If you see the Gandhi film, you will realise that it is the village in Indian English Novel, which is important and not the city. Our rural consciousness has not become city consciousness in spite of Americanization of Bombay and Delhi. It cannot because 90% of India is still the village folk, wanting participatory democracy.

All my work shows the collective unconscious of the land trying to become conscious of itself. The formulations of Gandhi, Tagore and Nehru point that way. And unless your students can bring out the village consciousness as emergent in the struggles of Rasta Roko etc. your proteges will remain aliens in India.

As for Mr. Vazirani, please write direct to him, asking if your book has sold any copies at all and are there any royalties due.

I wish you well with your American studies. Again I feel that, apart from the pioneer novelists Bret Harte, Hawthorne and others whom D.H. Lawrence dealt with, the contemporary Americans remain only of exotic interest to us, except Dos Passos, Faulkner, Richard Wright and the other blacks.

Currently, I am concentrating on writing my autobiography in whatever time I get from seminars.

With warm regards,

Yours sincerely,
Mulk Raj Anand

* * * * *

Bombay
January 20, 1983

Dear Ramakrishna,

This is to wish you all that you would like to wish for yourself in the New Year.

What I had in mind in my comments on the city business is something other than what most people say about the city. I am a student of Lewis Mumford and consider the coming of American style urbanism into our country as total abomination. Already the havoc on the life of the new young, growing up in skyscrapers, is terrible. And most Indian-English writers do not understand the kind of civilization Gandhi, Tagore and Jawaharlal Nehru wanted. They are imitating the urban literature of the West like Salman Rushdie! Too clever by half!

Regards,

Yours sincerely,
Mulk Raj Anand

* * * * *

Bombay
April 25, 1983

Dear Ramakrishna,

In between travel I have seen your note.

I suggest you immerse yourself in another art, or rather the art of the Deccan, from 6th century downwards, even if you want to write a fantasy. And tell Mr. S. Rao you can't dare to walk where angels fear to tread.

Also, about your *Quest*: unless you are as ruthless as Nirad Chaudhuri don't write. The academics are mostly derivative minds, aping the British or the Americans, with little or no honesty. Most of them want to put Tilak marks on everything and take cover behind Aurobindo to defend their confusions. They dare not be honest, like George Orwell or Malraux or even Cyril Connoly. And none of them have the calibre of Edmund Wilson in the *Axel's Castle*. No one with the courage of Henry Miller.

Try and write something like John Strachey's debunker of English intelligentsia before the war.

The failure of the Indian intelligentsia would be a good theme. Only you are a professor and might love your job, if you are honest.

Regards,

Yours sincerely,
Mulk Raj Anand

* * * * *

Bombay
May 10, 1983

Dear Ramakrishna,

A third person narrative is just invasion of personal experience. I have found that even the autobiographical novel put distance between myself and people and problems.

I am strictly for a personal statement, so I am writing a straightforward biography.

Regards,

Yours sincerely,
Mulk Raj Anand

* * * * *

Warangal
May 16, 1983

Dear Dr. Anand,

Thank you for your postcard of May 10. I'm indeed grateful to you for your continued encouragement in my efforts to "write." I have finally decided to complete the overdue project *The Quest*—an idea that came to me intensely on account of the stay at Banaras Hindu University during the 1960s. During those days that University appeared to be the only one affected. Since then, as you know, almost every Indian University is rocked, the latest being the JNU at New Delhi. This seems to have been an endless process on the Indian subcontinent. When can the powers-that-be stop it? Only when those powers are unsullied. And when can that paradise be regained?

My interest in these things is not merely academic. I have experienced intensely over the years and seen at close quarters many things that persons like you might have missed. For instance. I have known an Indian academic dismissing your work as "Leftist" (while talking to me) but flattering you when his own novel was due for publication. But what, what exactly, is responsible for the double standards? I do not know whether you are "Leftist" or not, but what has drawn me to you so much is the purely human side of your personality, as one associated with Mahatma Gandhi. Leftists are known for their contempt for Gandhi! Even after all these years, I am convinced that I have done the right thing.

I initially thought of third-person narrative only to maintain some distance from the characters and events portrayed. I wanted to avoid sounding like making too much of a personal statement.

Regards,

Yours sincerely,
D. Ramakrishna

* * * * *

Bombay
December 5, 1983

Dear friend,

Greetings of the season!

I returned from abroad about a fortnight ago, but had to go to Shantiniketan to preside over a seminar on Art.

I have seen the novel *The Unvan*.

As I anticipated it is shabbily produced and quite uninviting.

I feel so strongly in these matters, that I am asking Arnold-Heinemann to reprint *The Bubble* entirely, because it has been printed indifferently by Jaico Printers. Never mind the cost!

I am unhappy that the ambitions of young people to appear in print makes them impatient, too eager to see their words in print, and thus become the victims of the damn fool press in a small town, which will print their books.

I will try and overcome my feelings and read it as soon as I have some time.

I wonder why we Indians, with the ambition to write, can be so obtuse as to forget the wonderful books calligraphed by our ancients.

Somehow I feel personally hurt that all my labours in design and production of *Marg* books have been lost in Indian intelligentsia. No critic has noticed any of 134 volumes of *Marg* I produced during the last thirty years.

I went to Frankfurt fair and was ashamed to see that there was not one book from India well enough produced to compete with the productions of even a smallest publisher abroad.

What a fall my countrymen!

Regards,

Yours sincerely,
Mulk Raj Anand

* * * * *

Bombay
March 30, 1984

Dear friend Ramakrishna,

I have been dumbed by the killings in the North and am going about in the vain effort to arouse the intelligentsia to see our predicament as Indians, up against our own Mir Jafars and the enemies of promise from abroad.

I have done nothing else for months now.

I am going to London on a similar mission on Tuesday.

So I apologise for not writing to you any more than this brief note.

I think you are a sincere quester and will achieve much by pursing your search.

I believe, however, that any such writing should be in the first person singular, as in Raja Rao's novel and not in terms of the third person singular.

Unless there is a ruthless self-examination of ourselves, no quest can have authenticity, in my opinion.

Perhaps you will read *The Bubble* which is now out and may have had got to your University library. Why don't you review it?

This is written in a hurry.

Regards,

Yours sincerely,
Mulk Raj Anand

* * * * *

Warangal
April 7, 1984

Dear Dr. Anand,

Thank you very much for your kind letter of March 30.

Yes, the north is ablaze and the corridors of power in New Delhi are shaking. It's a pity the inhabitants of this "Karma Bhoomi," India, have transformed themselves into creatures lower than the animals, ironically enough in the name of religion too. Be it the killings by man in the north today or by Nature in Andhra a few years ago, you are sparing no efforts to persuade fellow human beings to see reason and to make life on this planet a cherished experience. Where politicians fail, writers and intelligentsia should make sincere efforts to succeed. But how many of our distinguished Indian writers are voicing such concern for the dignity of the human spirit? They stop with pious platitudes in writings and lectures (which mean money and publicity).

As for my *Quest*, kindly rest assured that I'm putting it in the first person. The scene shifts between two cities, Banaras and Hyderabad with which I have been involved for the past two decades. The book is not something concocted as a schoolboy's exercise but the recording of the intense soul-stirrings of one deeply involved in a quest for values. Instead of writing only autobiography, I'm trying to create some intellectual interest by synthesizing the concepts of education in the Upanishads, Plato, and Dewey—both the abstract and the concrete, the ideal and the real.

Yes, I'm reading your *Bubble* for review in *Littcrit* of Prof. P.K. Rajan. I shall send the review of that book as well as of K.V.S. Murthi's creative criticism *The Sword and the Sickle*.

Regards,

Yours sincerely,
D. Ramakrishna

P.S. I've read Khushwant Singh's review of *The Bubble*. Not so impressive!

* * * * *

Bombay
August 13, 1984

Dear good friend Ramakrishna,

I have just returned from Amritsar from what seems to me, in retrospect, a pilgrimage of pain. I found all of us are guilty, because we remained uninvolved and saw the rise of Rakshas without stirring out of our safe nests. I myself am guilty, because I did not go with Nirmal Deshpande on the Padayatra out of sheer cowardice, because I was on the hit list.

I found most of the Akalis more guilty because they know about the arms build-up and nothing about it. They even lied.

Now almost the whole Sikh intelligentsia is bitter and only talks of the events of 5th/6th June, without mentioning the desecration of Akal Takht by Bhindranwale and his Rakshas.

On the other hand, the South Indians seem not to care, what happens in the North. I suppose they will allow Rama Rao to parade himself as the heir of Tirupati Temple. There will be murders between Hindus and Muslims like in Hyderabad and they will sit by watching.

I wish some University people may notice the use of religion in politics. But I see that most of you are unconcerned.

I hope, after your present studies in literature are published, you will divert your mind by reading Malraux, Camus and Sartre, to see how the European contemporaries confronted the spiritual crises of their time.

I am again going North. Then to China on a Writers' delegation, which is a fruitless mission as the Chinese are in an open conspiracy with USA and Pakistan to weaken our frontiers.

Regards,

Yours sincerely,
Mulk Raj Anand

* * * * *

Bombay
October 5, 1985

Dear Ramakrishna,

I am reassured to hear from you, after a long time, that you are creatively busy.

I find myself involved in the education policy-making to the extent of writing memoranda on introducing creative education learning by doing.

This means being in Delhi almost half month.

I see some hope in the possible pooling of efforts through the new Resources Ministry. But the Babus are M.A.s, M.Sc.s without any imagination. And the men and women of imagination are following the existing I.A.S.-oriented syllabus.

I write my *Ap-biti* in between the formal work for the centre.

But, in this age of insensate violence, I don't think one should waste time on telling the hidebound Indian intelligentsia about the novel.

They will go imitating Jane Austen and E.M. Forster or Saul Bellow, when this land requires the inlook-outlook of people like Anthony Burgess or Alan Ginsberg.

Regards,

Yours sincerely,
Mulk Raj Anand

* * * * *

Bombay
October 18, 1985

Dear Ramakrishna,

I would like to know the name of the book reviewed by Meenakshi Mukherjee.

I believe there must be many more novels in India before one can issue a book of criticism—which means interpretation.

Currently, the Indian English writers write mostly about the English-speaking urbanites. They have hardly touched the collective unconscious of the folk, who do not speak in English. The bazaar culture of television, which represents the elite, must begin to express human interests of the people in the countryside.

If Tolstoy and Gorky could recreate Moujiks, the pandits of the intelligentsia, and the mother-tongue wallahs and the Indian English highbrows can get together and go to the people.

I am trying to explain in my autobiography how I was compelled to give voice to the silent. So, at the moment, I have no time for criticism, etc.

Regards,

Yours sincerely,
Mulk Raj Anand

* * * * *

Bombay
June, 11, 1996

Dear Dr. Ramakrishna,

Greetings and thank you for remembering me after all this time.

I am guilty about not having written in appreciation of your efforts to recall Poe. I have been having the aches and pains of the old age, but, importantly, concentrating on my novel, of the Gandhian struggle (or non-struggle) of 1927, already 1500 pages, about the unsuitable boy Gandhi as against the suitable boy of Vikram Seth!

As you can imagine it has become difficult for me to be as physically active as I have been even in the 80s. Now, there is a backache inevitable to the time when one has to bend before heaven for the privilege of being able to walk on the earth with a stick in hand.

I am afraid this physical disability to be active keeps me geared to my routine in my country place with small walks, body massage and a modest diet so that I can finish the seven volumes of my self-search novel.

I hope you will be able to come to some Seminar in Bombay or Pune, where we can meet or even perhaps Delhi.

Meanwhile, you might feel that you would like to review my reprint of *Conversations in Bloomsbury* published by OUP some months ago. Has your University library got it?

It has received one review from Khushwant Singh in two words, shameless name-dropping . . . but no professor of English has reacted to this seemingly superficial but important book in his motivations.

Warm regards,

Yours sincerely,
Mulk Raj Anand

* * * * *

Bombay
February 22, 1999

Dear Prof. Ramakrishna,

Greetings!

I was enthused into recall of our warm friendship of some years ago; I don't know why our communications were interrupted until now. . . .

I see that you have followed your obsession Edgar Allan Poe into further research which took you to USA!

I recall my feelings when I first read Poe's tales and then the wonderful essay on Poe by D.H. Lawrence in his passionate book on *Classic American Literature*.

I remember the inspiration from Lawrence, which made me read all the American Classics.

I hope you can communicate to your students your own enthusiasm, so that some of the young in India will know, beyond English Classics, the vital American novels which are surprisingly more vigorous than the mediaeval English fiction of Fielding, Smollett and Richardson!

I am ashamed, often, to find that even our Professors of English literature don't know the Classics of English literature and so produce half-baked M.A.s who become Ph.D.s and lecturers. And the general cultural background, say of Andhra is so inadequate that few teachers know that Ajanta paintings were done by Andhra craftsmen from 2nd century downwards.

I recall your initiative to correct my essays for which I had not yet time. I hope you can take up that collaboration again. But you may have to come here before we can do anything.

With warm regards,

Sincerely,
Mulk Raj Anand

* * * * *

Bombay
January 9, 2000

Dear Dr. Ramakrishna,

In going through my mail I find a long letter from you of 10th April, 1999. It is mainly about *Across the Black Waters*. You are the only critic who has taken any interest in this and my other fictions.

Meanwhile, the novel *Across the Black Waters* was adapted as a Play by a forward group in UK, and with help from British Council the play has been going round the Islands and ended up with a seminar at Birmingham.

I don't expect any such treatment of this novel from the Indian critics because in our hot country they are on a permanent siesta.

As for your own interest, the questionnaire is too long for me to answer.

I suggest the answers are in the novel itself.

Of course, I wrote it because some part of my father's Regiment went to the Western front 1200 from whom about 80 came back.

I toured the area in Alsace Lorraine and from my participation in Spanish War I wrote the novel which has been appreciated in the Commonwealth except in India. But then I expect the Indian professors to be very liberated in their awareness.

All that you need to know is in the novel itself and a review of it will answer my wish for it to be known.

Regards,

Yours sincerely,
Mulk Raj Anand

* * * * *

Bombay
January 15, 2000

Dear Dr. Ramakrishna,

I have been away from Mumbai for over a month and mail has been disturbed. The position is still the same.

Please bear with me!

Meanwhile, I am grateful for your article on *Across the Black Waters*.

As I told you, that novel was adapted as a Play and went on tour for eight months ending up in a Seminar in Birmingham in November.

Of course, any article on that novel might be more appreciated in UK or America than in India. Our intelligentsia seems to be subjective and has not shown interest in the International disasters which have implications for our country.

Apart from your article appearing in *Kakatiya Journal* it might also go to *Littcrit*. I will write again.

With warm regards,

Yours sincerely,
Mulk Raj Anand

* * * * *

Bombay
January 29, 2000

Dear Prof. Ramakrishna,

I appreciate very much the trouble you have taken to write a whole critique on my novel *Across the Black Waters*—the only Indian essay in appreciation of what has been honoured in U.K. I have misplaced the text you sent me; so please send me a copy of the same.

And perhaps you could send one to *Frontline* Magazine, address to Shri Ram, who is a brilliant editor.

Please forgive me for the muddle but I am in the country and not in Bombay. So filing is not done properly.

With kind regards,

Yours sincerely,
Mulk Raj Anand

* * * * *

Bombay
February 14, 2000

Dear Dr. Ramakrishna,

I am grateful for your prompt dispatch of the article, *Across the Black Waters*.

I am reassured that you sent a copy to Shri N. Ram, editor of *Frontline*, as his journal is the only likely one to notice a literary event of this significance, which *Across the Black Waters* has achieved through its own momentum.

While I easily welcome new initiatives by writers in Indian English, there are still people like Dr. Naik concerned about who is Indian and who is not. By which they mean who is reviving Hindutva and who is against belated religious chauvinism.

Anyhow thank you for your patience and attention.

Warm regards,

Sincerely,
Mulk Raj Anand

Nissim Ezekiel

Bombay
August 21, 1977

Dear Dr. Ramakrishna,

Thank you for your letter of 17 August. I am glad you enjoy reading *Freedom First* and respond to my editorials. The journal needs lots more subscribers and support if it is to survive.

Congratulations on the good reviews of your anthology in the journals you mention. Is there any way of reading them? The cuttings could be returned.

Regards,

Yours sincerely,
Nissim Ezekiel

* * * * *

Warangal
August 23, 1977

Dear Mr. Ezekiel,

Thank you for your note of the 21st of August.

Since my subject is "Ezekiel's Literary Creed," I will be largely dealing with your statements outside your poetry. Of course, that should be done after an understanding of your poetry, as you say. So I reserve the general questions to the future.

As a beginning, a few minor queries:

i) Your poem "Goodbye Party for Miss Pushpa T.S.," is often quoted in poetry gatherings. I heard you also fondly reading it once in Hyderabad. Could one draw the conclusion that the predominant note of your poetry is humorous, coming as it does after all that disillusionment with urban life in poems like "A Morning Walk," "Urban," and "Enterprise"? Or, does it mean that you are one of those "self-conscious Indo-Anglian poets" (as Meenakshi Mukherjee puts it) who are more concerned with the response to the English language rather than to the urgent need to communicate a perception?

ii) As a craftsman, you are known for the meticulous care taken in the construction of your poems. What do you think of Poe's "The Philosophy of Composition" which describes a poem as a "mathematical" construction? Do you subscribe to Poe's Principle or to the inspiration theory?

iii) Did you have T.S. Eliot in mind while writing pieces like "A Morning Face" and "Enterprise"?

iv) Don't you think that in your preoccupation with the urban characters, you have ignored a major segment of the Indian life, the rural folks? Have you depicted the confrontation of the urban and the rural cultures, which is so vital an aspect of the Indian culture? Or, do you say that you, as a poet, are more concerned with an exploration of your self lost in the "Barbaric city rich with slums. . . ./ A million purgatorial lanes?"

Kindly enlighten me on these small points.

Best regards,

Yours sincerely,
D. Ramakrishna

* * * * *

Bombay
August 27, 1977

Dear Mr. Ramakrishna,

This is in reply to your letter of 23 August.

I shall merely answer your questions—very briefly:

1) "Goodbye Party" is one of five or six poems in Indian English. How can any one talk of predominant note etc. on the basis of such few poems of a certain kind or jump to conclusions about "self-conscious Indo-Anglian poets," I don't know. My interests and concerns have to be judged from the whole or a substantial part of my work.

2) I don't believe a poem is a "mathematical" construction. I don't subscribe to Poe's or any other principle. I am particularly against extremist and dogmatic theories of how poetry is written.

3) No, I didn't have T.S. Eliot in mind when I wrote "A Morning Walk" and "Enterprise." There are poems of the kind that were being written in England at the time, the 1950s and 1960s.
4) I write what I can and not what I should. The demand that urban poets should write about rural situations or rural poets about urban matters is all wrong in my view.

Regards,

Yours sincerely,
Nissim Ezekiel

* * * * *

Bombay
October 1, 1977

Dear Friend,

The interview was tape-recorded. The answers were intended to stand as they are, except for minor revisions. My answers to your questions are merely an aid to your formulations. You may of course quote but in essence you will be speaking in your voice, to explain, interpret, criticise mine. That's the difference I've been trying to convey to you.

Anyway, I will answer your questions as best as I can and then leave it to you to work out your proposed article.

With best wishes,

Yours sincerely,
Nissim Ezekiel

* * * * *

Bombay
October 8, 1977

Dear Friend,

This is in reply to your postcard of October 4th and my last communication for the present. Glad you are getting more and more material of the kind you sought. As you rightly say, you shouldn't overplay the game. It's the actual critical argument that finally matters.

I leave for Hawaii on 14th October, shall be back on 2nd November.

Regards,

Yours sincerely,
Nissim Ezekiel

* * * * *

Warangal
November 22, 1977

Dear Mr. Ezekiel,

I hope you are back in Bombay after a successful trip to Hawaii.

I have received the xerox copy of your *Quest* article on "Poetry as Knowledge." The ASRC people couldn't get the piece on "Poetry as Philosophy." Birje has sent me his piece on you published in CDN's journal. Also I have got a copy of the Osmania University special number on Indian Poetry in English.

But I don't like to retell the story told by all these people. I want something from the horse's mouth, as they put it. Hence I'm completing the exhaustive questionnaire. Just a specimen here:

> It's somewhat difficult to appreciate your poetry, including the poster poems, without an insight into art. So is the case with some of the major English poets like Robert Browning. Even though there is not much of the dramatic quality in your poetry as in Browning's, nevertheless there is in much of your poetry an imaginative harmonization of background as in the Victorian poet's lyrics and monologues. In "The Last Ride Together" and "Cleon," Browning says life is greater than art. In "Andrea del Sarto," he tries to establish the supremacy of art. In "Transcendentalism" the poet says that the object of poetry is the presentation of life in concrete terms. "Look you," he says, referring to the rose,
>
> Song's our art
> Whereas you please to speak these naked thoughts
> Instead of draping them in sights and sounds.

How do you react to the fusion of the dramatic and the artistic in Browning's poetry? Do you think you achieve such a synthesis in your own poetry?

I look forward to hearing from you.

With warm regards,

Yours sincerely,
D. Ramakrishna

* * * * *

Bombay
November 11, 1977

Dear Mr. Ramakrishna,

I don't quite understand what you mean when you say that it is difficult to appreciate my poetry "without an insight into art." Do you mean technique? If so, certainly any poet is better understood by insights into his technique. But a first or rudimentary understanding is possible without much awareness of technical devices used by the poet. In my case, that is certainly so, as even the most complex of my poems are relatively simple and direct, judged by the norms of different poetry properly so-called.

The phrase "imaginative harmonization of background" appeals to me. I hope it is true of my poetry to some extent.

I am not basically in sympathy with Browning's temperament or credo. But the fusion of the dramatic and the artistic in his poetry I consider largely successful. Browning makes a big thing out of it. My poetry cannot be compared to his in terms of art but I don't make a big thing out of any method of approach to poetry and life. Mine has been, so far, a modest way in poetry, in accordance with my estimate of my talents.

To the extent I have used dramatic techniques, they have been unobtrusive, minor ways of enriching the poem. "Synthesis" is too ambitious a word in application to my poetry, but neither is my poetry a mere hodgepodge of devices and lyrical emotions. I work carefully to be appropriate, to maintain a tone, to prevent anomalies or incongruities.

In general life is and has to be greater than art, preceding it and retaining its primacy. By "supremacy of art" one only means to assert its necessity, indispensability for living in the full sense of living. One does not mean that it is or should be treated as of greater value than life.

Yours sincerely,
Nissim Ezekiel

* * * * *

Bombay
May 28, 1978

Dear Mr. Ramakrishna,

Thank you for your letter, received in Bangalore. I am enclosing a poem written there. You have probably read or read enough about *Roots* to appreciate the sentiment of the poem.

I have not written much of value or even interest on American life and literature. There are only a few papers written for academic and instructional seminars. So Dr. Lohof will not be able to put together anything likely to be useful to you. As for the "American aspect of my credo" I shall wait for your interpretation before making any comment.

Regards,

Sincerely,
Nissim Ezekiel

* * * * *

Warangal
June 5, 1978

Dear Mr. Ezekiel,

Thank you for your note of May 28 and the enclosed poem entitled "After Reading *Roots*." Yes, I have read *Roots* with great interest and been engaged in some sort of a cultural exploration myself. That's what has prompted me to embark on an integration of "American Studies" and "Indian English Studies" (if the overlords of Indian English Writing permit me to indulge in such usage.) One of the objectives of my study of your "credo" is to analyse such cross-cultural experience.

I have received from Dr. Lohof a xerox copy of your "Personal Review of T.S. Eliot" published in 1965. From the purely academic point of view, you have said nothing new in that essay. Nevertheless, it is of some interest to me from the "creative" point of view since I could study a few of your assertions in respect of Eliot and the creative process. In one of your letters to me a few months ago, you had denied any special admiration for Eliot. I have now got some evidence to disprove that denial! You know that Walt Whitman disowned any influence of the Indian philosophy. However, modern Whitman specialists, as sophisticated as Gay Wilson Allen and James E. Miller, are convinced that there are definite traces of Indian mysticism in Whitman's poetry. These things happen in respect of all creative writers.

The reference to your views on Eliot is but an aspect of your "Americanness." It's possible to discover more interesting facts in your writings on contemporary American poetry published in SPAN and *Reviews in American Studies*. I have been attempting a similar exploration in regard to a few other major Indian writers in English. If, however, they tell me publicly or privately that they admire the American dollar more than the American genius, I am helpless!

Your recent poem, "After Reading *Roots*," is an illustration of the basic tension in you between the academic and the creative artist. By responding to a popular book, you have expressed your shock at a distressing contemporary cultural situation. It will be heartening if you could respond to the contemporary Indian situation with deeper involvement.

I trust that your recent poetry proves a major breakthrough in your creative effort, disproving the rulings of some Indian scholars that Nissim Ezekiel, "Our once 'major' poet," (*Osmania Journal of English Studies* [Contemporary Indian Poetry in English Special Number] 1977: 64) is now worth relegating to the archives!

Best regards,

Yours sincerely,
D. Ramakrishna

* * * * *

Bombay
December 18, 1978

Dear Mr. Ramakrishna,

Glad to know of your assignment and best wishes for it. Don't think I have any off-the-cuff advice to offer at this early stage. If specific issues arise, as they are bound to, on which you seek comments, certainly I shall make mine.

The question of removing your name from the PEN mailing list did not arise. The organisation is not run on an arbitrary personal basis. When your cheque arrives, I shall do as you suggest. Thanks. Nice to know you like my article in *The Indian PEN*.

I note what you say about your proposed essay on my "credo." Miss Clark has been a good friend all these years and I am not surprised at her interest in your essay on me. I posted to you separately a *New Quest* reprint, and my latest sequence of poems.

Reciprocated greetings for the season and the new year.

With regards,

Yours faithfully,
Nissim Ezekiel

* * * * *

Warangal
December 28, 1978

Dear Prof. Ezekiel,

It's almost impossible to sustain oneself as a full-time creative writer—even in the States—for reasons well known. Nevertheless, I think the University career has its own compensatory aspects for writers, both in India and abroad. The writer knows his critics!

Isaac was here this morning. We were talking about you at my place and in the meantime your note of Dec. 24, together with the *Fulcrum* clipping, reached me. It's a very useful piece indeed.

Next month I will spend a few days at the CIEFL, researching for my anthology. If I find the libraries in Hyderabad inadequate, I shall go to Madras too.

Isaac told me that you would be in Hyderabad in February for the Sarojini Devi Seminar. I hope it would be possible for us to meet either in Hyderabad or in Warangal. Prof. Sisir Kumar Ghose writes to me that he would be attending the Seminar.

With warm regards,

Yours sincerely,
D. Ramakrishna

* * * * *

Bombay
February 6, 1979

Dear Mr. Ramakrishna,

I feel that the prose piece may be most suitable for your proposed anthology is "Naipaul's India and Mine" which is a review of *An Area of Darkness*. It first appeared in "Imprint" magazine and then in Adil Jussawalla's *New Writing from India* (Penguin).

I've never thought very highly of Frank Moraes's prose style but the last chapter of his biography of Nehru may well be suitable for your prose anthology. Dom, of course, writes very elegantly, both prose and verse.

With best wishes,

Yours faithfully,
Nissim Ezekiel

* * * * *

Bombay
April 19, 1979

Dear Friend,

Soon after I wrote to you, I received a review of Shiv Kumar's novel. The reviewer informs me that I had agreed to this personally through Dr. Chirantan Kulshrestha of the University of Hyderabad. I don't remember this, but it must be so. In the circumstances I would like you to let me use your review for *The Journal of English Studies*, edited by D.S. Velayudhan from Tellicherry. I am the journal's poetry editor, but I also help it obtain other material.

I hope you will agree to this, and I shall then inform Dr. Velayudhan accordingly.

I have with me *The Peace which Passeth Understanding*, a study of *The Waste Land* by Dr. G. Nageswara Rao, published by Sri Venkateswara University, Tirupati. Would you care to review this for *The Indian PEN*? If not, I'll make another suggestion later.

With best wishes,

Yours faithfully,
Nissim Ezekiel

* * * * *

Bombay
April 26, 1979

Dear Ramakrishna,

Yes, I've written to Dr. S. Velayudhan to clear your review. When I hear from him, I'll confirm the arrangement. Would you like to review Bhabani Bhattacharya's latest novel, *A Dream in Hawaii*? If you say yes, I'll post it to you. The novel is in 245 pages of a paperback edition.

Thanks,

Yours sincerely,
Nissim Ezekiel

* * * * *

Bombay
June 16, 1979

Dear Mr. Ramakrishna,

I've noted all you say in your letter of 13 June. Take your time over the review of *A Dream in Hawaii*. It's good that there is a prospect of your writing for *The Indian Express*. I presume the prose anthology, which you don't mention this time, is either complete or awaiting only a few items and clearances.

Best wishes,

Yours sincerely,
Nissim Ezekiel

* * * * *

Bombay
October 6, 1979

Dear Dr. Ramakrishna,

Thank you for your newsy letter, which was a pleasure to read. Congratulations on all the good things that have happened to you and the others that are about to happen. I'm glad your library has ordered the new Clearing House books. I am looking forward to *Cygnus*.

You've made good use of Bhattacharya's novel. The review for *The Indian PEN* could reach us by the end of this month, if that's convenient to you. Let's hope the prose anthology is published in London instead of in Delhi. It sounds very substantial, from your description and I'm sure it will be an indispensable source book for the study of Indian Writing in English.

You probably know that Oxford University Press is reprinting its Indian Poetry series. They have also offered me a new book for publication next year. I'm putting the manuscript together.

Best wishes,

Yours sincerely,
Nissim Ezekiel

* * * * *

Bombay
June 3, 1980

Dear Friend,

Thank you for your letter of 14th May. It must have arrived after I left for Bangalore on 17th May, returning at the end of the month.

I saw the leaflet announcing your anthology and await a copy of the book. No request for an article has come to me from Allied Publishers. I don't know who is editing their anthology and what its scope is.

I've started editing an old political monthly entitled *Freedom First* since February. A specimen issue of the latest issue is being posted to you separately.

With best wishes,

Yours sincerely,
Nissim Ezekiel

* * * * *

Warangal
June 17, 1980

Dear Professor Ezekiel,

I have just returned from my hometown after a brief vacation following the completion of my work on *Indian-English Prose: An Anthology*. The book (332 pp. in hard cover) will be out by the end of this month. It's now at the binding stage.

Together with your letter of June 3, I received the specimen copy of the latest issue of *Freedom First*. I have read the issue with interest. You have set an example to the Indo-English poets by actively participating in the contemporary life. A new definition to the writer's role in society! Perhaps the journal's scope will be wider if it regularly publishes articles on the theme, "writer and society." How many of our Indo-English poets have expressed their agony at the state of the country even as Tennyson and Arnold did in the Victorian age?

With warm regards,

Yours sincerely,
D. Ramakrishna

* * * * *

Bombay
June 25, 1980

Dear Friend,

Glad to hear about the book. I look forward to a copy, and also, if you can manage it, a review copy for *Freedom First*.

I'm pleased that you approve of my political involvement. Thank you for your suggestion that I should publish some articles on the Writer and Society. I'll try to get some on various aspects of this theme.

In India, after getting a book published one cannot wait for it to make its own way. One has to push it along. I'm afraid that's what you'll have to do if the anthology of Indian English prose is to be widely reviewed and to make an impact. You need have no inhibitions on that score. And I shall certainly be happy to help, at least in Bombay.

With best wishes,

Yours sincerely,
Nissim Ezekiel

* * * * *

Bombay
July 5, 1980

Dear Friend,

I have your letter (26th June) and the postcard (28th June). I shall certainly do what I can to promote your anthology of prose. I'm looking forward to a copy. A review will certainly appear in *Freedom First* and in *Kavi* when review copies arrive. I shall not hold it against the book if certain pieces are included which may not satisfy my judgement. I can quite appreciate your point of view.

I'm glad to know that your book on Poe is being reconsidered for publication. I do hope you get that post-doctoral Fulbright.

I'll write to you soon after I receive copies of the anthology, my own and the review copies. These will help me start promoting the book—AIR, Television and the local newspapers / journals.

Regards,

Yours sincerely,
Nissim Ezekiel

* * * * *

Bombay
August 29, 1980

Dear Friend,

I had heard about the anthology's appearance from your colleague Dr. P. Shiv Kumar. Congratulations. I'm glad Mr. Vazirani has already sent me a copy. It should soon be in my hands. I shall certainly do all I can to promote it. For this purpose some extra copies are essential. Once I part with my copy, I often lose it for ever.

Regards and best wishes,

Yours sincerely,
Nissim Ezekiel

* * * * *

Bombay
September 23, 1980

Dear Friend,

Soon after writing to you last, I received a copy of your *Indian-English Prose: Anthology*. This was addressed to me as Editor of *Freedom First* and the book is for review. Am I not to get a copy even as contributor?

As for Chirantan's anthology, the publisher has sent me a bill for the second copy which I did not ask for.

Regards,

Yours sincerely,
Nissim Ezekiel

* * * * *

Bombay
October 1, 1980

Dear Friend,

I wrote you a postcard when your book arrived. Thanks. I note that copies have been sent to Nandy and Mrs. Zakaria. I shall speak to the latter about it.

A receipt for your *Freedom First* subscription is enclosed. I've been speaking to friends about the kind of contribution you have suggested but don't envisage a regular feature.

I'm glad you are concentrating now on the Poe manuscript. Publication of that will certainly be a major event in your intellectual life.

Regards and best wishes.

Yours sincerely,
Nissim Ezekiel

* * * * *

Warangal
April 29, 1981

Dear Professor Ezekiel,

I hope you have received my note from the ASRC in the second week of this month. *Freedom First* (April 1981) has just reached me. It's remarkable that you have kept up your attacks on the corrupt state of the Indian democracy in your anxiety to spread the message of true freedom of man. However, instead of ending up at the level of these editorials and other things connected with politics, you should be able to do greater service to the Muse of Indian English poetry by spreading the message of democracy through your creative writing in the style of a Whitman. Whitman too, as you know, was for some time involved in practical politics but subsequently made the best creative use of the involvement.

I have also received the latest issue of the *IJAS* containing your piece on the contemporary American Poetry. Even though the present essay is not in the same critical vein as was evident in the articles you had written for the *Reviews in American Studies* at my invitation, you have nevertheless shown your continuing interest in the subject.

I have no doubt that in the years to come your creative activity will be much wider since only that can ultimately provide the necessary outlet for a genius of your standing. Involvement with Indian politicians, to whatever ideology they belong, may eventually lead to disillusionment for the genuine creative writer.

With kind regards,

Yours sincerely,
D. Ramakrishna

* * * * *

Bombay
May 8, 1981

Dear Friend,

I appreciate the spirit of your letter (29th April). The note you refer to from the ASRC seems to elude my memory. Perhaps you could post me a copy.

I should certainly attempt writing the kind of political poetry you hint at. Whether I can bring it off is another matter but certainly I would like to try. At the moment I do seem to need some more immediate connection with the political scene, and *Freedom First* provides it, in spite of its limitations.

With regards,

Yours sincerely,
Nissim Ezekiel

* * * * *

Bombay
September 22, 1981

Dear Ramakrishna,

Thank you for your postcard of 14th Sept.

I've received Professor Ayyappa Paniker's review of your anthology in *Littcrit*. It goes without saying that the number of positive reviews of it will increase. I'm glad you reminded me that I had promised to promote the book. I shall take it up in suitable ways, and hope to get results by the end of the year.

I'm glad to know you are making progress with your study of Poe's empiricism.

Regards,

Yours sincerely,

Nissim Ezekiel

* * * * *

Bombay
October 24, 1981

Dear Ramakrishna,

Thank you for giving me so much news about yourself, all of it good. No, we don't get *World Literature Today*. I would welcome a copy of the review if you can have it made.

It does seem that many demands are being made on your time. But the article on Indo-English prose could have been a personal one—regarding the making of the anthology and the reactions to it.

Best wishes for the completion of the Poe book.

Regards,

Yours sincerely,
Nissim Ezekiel

* * * * *

Warangal
February 7, 1982

Dear Prof. Ezekiel,

I have just received *Freedom First* and quite enjoyed reading it. Under the caption "A Variety of Comment" you have introduced non-political issues too. A couple of years ago, I had suggested that you invite the creative writers to express their views about Indian society and politics. Eventually, such frank views expressed in a journal like yours may serve as source material relating to those writers. What I have been saying is that the writer in you need not entirely be dissociated from the social and political commentator. You need not, of course, end up as a mere "political writer"!

Regards,

Yours sincerely,
D. Ramakrishna

* * * * *

Bombay
February 20, 1982

Dear Friend,

I agree with all you say in your letter (postcard) of 7/2/82. It is a kind of failure on my part that I could not get the non-political yet relevant articles I needed for *Freedom First*. I agree that I should not be merely a "political writer." I shall remember your warning.

Hope all is well with you.

Regards,

Yours sincerely,
Nissim Ezekiel

* * * * *

Bombay
January 18, 1983

Dear Friend,

I replied to your previous letter at the ASRC, Hyderabad.

Glad to know of your progress on the proposed criticism anthology. Best of luck. Of course, there is the city in the Indo-English novel. It's not all rural culture, as you say.

Yes, I was invited to the Gyan Bagh Palace during my stay in Hyderabad for the "social" seminar as you call it, along with a select number of delegates and others.

It was quite enjoyable.

Hope we meet before the end of 1983!

Regards,

Yours sincerely,
Nissim Ezekiel

* * * * *

Bombay
September 15, 1983

Dear Friend,

Good to hear the news of your work.

Best wishes for the Poe book. I'm sure the ASRC anthology will be a good one.

About Mr. Sudhakar Rao novel, I shall certainly read his MSS. But I must confess I can no longer cope with MSS on the scale I once did. And they tend to accumulate with me, to be neglected or not followed up in terms of publication. I shall manage to make a critical comment or two, that's all.

I returned two days ago from a three-week visit to the UK, two in Edinburgh, one in London. I had to read my poems at the Book Festival, and also gave a reading in London. It was pleasant and rewarding. I must soon write my letters of thanks, though!

Regards,

Yours sincerely,
Nissim Ezekiel

* * * * *

Bombay
September 27, 1983

Dear Friend,

Your postcard. Thanks for the feeling expressed about my poetry and the Edinburgh visit. I expect to post you in a week or so my *Edinburgh Interlude*, 30 times in a sequence written from 10th Aug. to 12th Sept. the three-week phase in the U.K.

Glad you liked the *Span* interview. You may certainly count on me to co-operate with you in the writing of the proposed essay on my "credo," as you call it. I shall willingly answer any questions you put me. As for material, you mention the *Hymns*. That was published in December, 1976. Surely you have a copy. The *Latter-Day Psalms* volume was released in the UK during my visit but in Bombay in December, 1982 during the All-India English Teachers Conference. You may even have it in your University library, and if you don't, the library may order not only my book but the other two in the same series, "New Poetry from India," released by the Oxford University Press. Let me know the situation.

Best wishes,

Yours sincerely,
Nissim Ezekiel

* * * * *

Bombay
May 12, 1984

Dear Dr. Ramakrishna,

Yes, I did receive your letter about the Indian representation in your Anthology, and await developments.

In response to your questions, my interest in art is reflected rather rarely in my poetry but I've never tried to spot its occurrences. Some reader of my verse may do so. Art is relevant to poetry but obliquely, not in some ideological way. One does not expect direct references to paintings or sculpture though they may in fact occur. Art is relevant as the broader concept within which poetry is included, just as a poet may sometimes be described as a true artist.

I've not noticed much direct influence of modern art on Indo-English poetry but still I'm sure there is some such influence and it could be traced.

Yes, I noticed the irony of the article on the Lalit Kala below my piece. The new man in charge is very unconvincing.

Regards,

Yours sincerely,
Nissim Ezekiel

* * * * *

Bombay
November 7, 1984

Dear Dr. Ramakrishna,

The LSD experience was not regarded by me as pseudo-religious. It seemed religious though I had some reservations about it later in terms of practice, actual religious practice as against religious consciousness.

Regards,

Yours sincerely,
Nissim Ezekiel

* * * * *

Bombay
July 23, 1985

Dear Friend,

In view of what you say in your letter of 19th July, you may send along your article for the special issue. Even if your book with the article in it appears a little earlier than the special issue, we shall treat it as an exception. I would like this question not to come in the way of your publication's appearance. I have informed Miss Anklesaria accordingly and she agrees.

When you meet Damodar convey my congratulations to him on his Doctorate.

And congratulations to you on all your intellectual activities.

I read your review in the April 1985 issue of the ILR.

If you write to Dr. Schendler, convey my best wishes to him for his total recovery.

Regards,

Yours sincerely,
Nissim Ezekiel

* * * * *

Bombay
27 September, 1985

Dear Friend,

Thank you for your letter of 20 September. I look forward to your article, and shall edit it carefully. I appreciate your granting me the freedom to make the cuts and changes I consider necessary.

I feel the publication of your book should not be delayed because one chapter is now scheduled for use in the proposed special issue on me. After all, that issue itself may be delayed, one never knows. It would be best to go ahead with your plans for the book, and if the special issue comes later, I shall still make sure your article appears in it.

Regards,

Yours sincerely,
Nissim Ezekiel

* * * * *

Bombay
June 13, 1986

Dear Friend,

Thank you for your letter of the 8th. I leave for Singapore tomorrow midnight, return 29th, leave for the U.K. on 4th July, return end of the month, and so on. . . . The autobiography or autobiographical novel you suggest will obviously have to wait!

The special issue of the *Journal of Indian Writing in English* is in press, and the proofs of two sections have been corrected.

The issue is expected by the end of July. I shall inquire about offprints.

Regards,

Yours sincerely,
Nissim Ezekiel

* * * * *

Bombay
August 31, 1986

Dear Friend,

I returned this afternoon after a week in Poona University and read your postcard of the 27th. I'm sure you have by now received a copy of the special issue with your article in it, prominently placed. The editor was provided with all the contributors' addresses.

I've asked an ex-student to review *Close Encounters* but haven't yet received the review for appropriate placing. I shall follow this up soon. An announcement will appear in *The Indian PEN*, next issue which will be (alas!) dated Nov.-Dec. 1985. We are dropping the 1986 issues and resuming publication with quarterly in 1987.

With best wishes,

Yours sincerely,
Nissim Ezekiel

* * * * *

Bombay
April 6, 1987

Dear Friend,

Sorry for the delay in replying to your letter of 16th March. Glad to know about your activities and movements. I look forward to the publication of your Poe thesis. Regarding your essay on my credo, perhaps Perry did like it, since even Americans sometimes mean what they say!

So far as I can remember, *The Indian PEN* did, in one of its long-delayed issues, announce your *Encounters*. Unfortunately, I can't trace the issue in which it appeared but expect to do so eventually. I also gave the book to an ex-student for review, and it was published in the Free Press Journal, cutting from which is enclosed.

With regards,

Yours sincerely,
Nissim Ezekiel

* * * * *

ASRC, Hyderabad
May 20, 1987

Dear Friend,

Thank you for your letter of the 18th. I'm glad to know that the cassette is a success. If I'm in India at the time of the CIEFL conference on American Literature, I shall certainly attend it. Dr. Bhalla has invited me, even if I don't read a paper.

You say you have scores of points to raise about my poetry, which you will do when we meet again. You could send me a few at a time, half a dozen or so, and I will send you my replies in writing. You may then use them in any way you choose or even keep them unused, for your personal interest.

With regards,

Yours sincerely,
Nissim Ezekiel

* * * * *

ASRC, Hyderabad
December 29, 1987

Dear Ramakrishna,

Thank you for your letter of the 23rd.

Reciprocated good wishes to you and yours for 1988.

About Indo-English poetry, let's hope the situation changes radically both in terms of the new generation and the new performance of the earlier ones. If it is considered "slender" at present, the critics' responsibility, I suppose, is to describe and analyse the slenderness, not merely to throw the word around as a label.

I've always been interested in translation from the regional languages into English. But the results of my interest have been meagre. Maybe I should try again to start a new project relating to it.

What can one think of a poet who is "angry" because he is "sandwiched" in a book of interviews between two poets of whom he doesn't think highly? He is obviously very small-minded.

Krishna Srinivas and circle give away those Hon. D.Litt. degrees.

Regards,

Yours sincerely,
Nissim Ezekiel

* * * * *

Bombay
May 22, 1988

Dear Friend,

This is in partial response to your letter of the 18th. It concerns only your project of editing the Telugu books of Seshendra Sarma's in English translation by himself.

I wonder if you could consider forwarding to me two or three of these poems for publication in *The Indian PEN*. Also, if you can send me a copy of your 10-page comments on his MSS (Indo-English Poetry and its criticism).

Regards,

Yours sincerely,
Nissim Ezekiel

* * * * *

Bombay
June 3, 1988

Dear Friend,

After my provisional postcard message in reply to your letter of 18th May, I thought I would deal at some length with your question: "I trust each time you go out of India on poetry-reading tours, you are able to return to your homeland with new ideas. What's your latest experience?"

Now I find I can't really deal with this, either in relation to the recent Australia/New Zealand trip in March or any other in the present perspective.

This may be because I feel I may have new ideas but unless I can show them realised in practice (specific poems), I should not spin out my theories. So, for the present, I'll let the question remain unanswered.

Regards,

Yours sincerely,
Nissim Ezekiel

* * * * *

Bombay
June 6, 1988

Dear Friend,

Just received your letter of the 2nd. Thanks for writing so fully about matters of our mutual interest. I look forward to a few translations by you of smaller poems by Seshendra Sarma for publication in *The Indian PEN*.

When you get back your carbon copy of the commentary on Perry's MSS., I know you will send it on to me. I'll have it xeroxed and return your carbon copy promptly. By the way, could you let me have his present address? It would be great for Indo-English poetry and allied subjects to have collaboration projects between the two of you. I can't help feeling that in the long run they may pay off better than the Poe writings. And I say this knowing how much they mean to you, quite rightly.

I've sent off today to the Oxford University Press the MSS of my collected poems, hoping the promised hardcover edition will be out in a year or so.

In the meanwhile, I plan to work on my plays, old and new. On 19th August I shall present a reading of my only tragedy, *Soft and Sad Music* at the British Council Auditorium. I've already given one reading of it for the Bombay English Association.

With regards,

Yours sincerely,
Nissim Ezekiel

* * * * *

Bombay
August 4, 1988

Dear Friend,

Thank you for your letter of 28 July. I remember asking for your comments on Perry's MSS but I have *not* received them. If

I had, I would certainly have sent you my reactions, and the original carbon copy.

I will publish Mr. Sarma's poems in the Oct.-Dec. '88 issue of *The Indian PEN*. Would it be OK to say 'Translated from the Telugu by the poet'? I shall also need his address eventually so that I may inform him about the acceptance of his poems, sent by you, for publication in *The Indian PEN* and in due course copies of the journal.

With gratitude for your co-operation and best wishes,

Yours sincerely,
Nissim Ezekiel

* * * * *

Bombay
August 15, 1988

Dear Friend,

Thank you for your letter of the 6th, with the address of Seshendra Sarma and other information. As for the comments on Perry's MSS, I do really want to read them. If you don't have a copy, I can only hope that in due course you will have one, perhaps from Perry himself, wherever he may be at present. Till then, don't worry about it.

The production of *Marriage Poem* at the Alliance Francaise did rather well. I'm now waiting for the Reading of *Don't Call It Suicide* at the British Council on the 19th.

Regards,

Yours sincerely,
Nissim Ezekiel

* * * * *

Bombay
August 27, 1988

Dear Friend,

Received your letter of the 20th with a xerox copy of your comments on Perry's MSS. Once I've read it I shall return it so that anyone else interested may get it from you, as I have, gratefully. If Perry comments on your comments I would like to be kept informed, if possible.

I wonder when Perry's MSS will be published.

With regards,

Yours sincerely,
Nissim Ezekiel

PS: I here acknowledge also your letter of the 18th with your kind advice and suggestions.

* * * * *

Bombay
October 25, 1988

Dear Friend,

Thanks for all the news in your letter of the 21st. It may be a good idea to try EXCHANGE first for your article. You know that I leave for Singapore on 1st December. Before that I expect to attend the All-India English Teachers Conference at Kolhapur: 24/26 November.

Glad to know that Perry will be back in India to continue work on his book. You may find a special way of collaborating with him, since he has already completed 7 chapters. You could be his critic and advisor.

In due course, I hope to read your paper on "Multiculturality and Indian English Writing."

Regards,

Yours sincerely,
Nissim Ezekiel

* * * * *

Bombay
June 15, 1991

Dear Dr. Ramakrishna,

Thank you for your letter of 3rd June and your appreciation of *The Indian PEN*. I would certainly welcome your contributions to it on Indian Literature.

Congratulations on all your achievements in the field of American fiction. Hope you will be able to accept the invitations of Prof. Lasley Dameron and Bob Crunden.

If Prof. V.K. Chari would be interested, I shall be glad to arrange a PEN lecture by him on Sanskrit criticism or some allied subject. It could be in late July or early August, a Monday or a

Thursday preceded by a Reception at 5.30 p.m. (Lecture at 6.15 p.m.)

Unfortunately, we cannot meet any expenses nor pay our speakers.

Let me know.

Regards,

Yours sincerely,
Nissim Ezekiel

Nayantara Sahgal

Warangal
July 8, 1978

To
Mrs. Nayantara Sahgal
New Delhi.

Dear Mrs. Sahgal,

I have recently read with interest your novel *A Situation in New Delhi*, and been in the process of writing an article on the novel for the 'Indian English Novel' special number of our research publication. As I am meditating on the shape my ideas should take, your article entitled "Stuck in the Status Quo" has appeared in *The Indian Express* of today. In your recent novel too all the tension between tradition and change in the Indian society is excellently portrayed. Devi stands for some sort of tradition in the eyes of the hot-blooded youth Rishad but in Devi herself is a conflict between the traditional Indian womanhood and the modern blonde. Perhaps she is more modern than traditional. Perhaps it is this chaotic condition between tradition and change that one finds in Indian life today.

It will be of immense help to me if you could kindly answer the following questions:

1. In describing lives of characters like Devi you seem to be trying to bring out both the change that has come to Indian womanhood and the corresponding tension. What is your opinion about the average Indian woman? As you know, very few Indian women have had the opportunity to get into the glittering social atmosphere of a metropolitan city.
2. While sketching the lives of politicians and officials in your fiction, you seem to be trying to expose the utter hollowness

of the systems in which they are functioning. What do you think of the intelligentsia among those at the helm of affairs? Intelligentsia need not necessarily mean the helpless Indian university and college professors. Among politicians and officials too there are individuals who stand between practical politics and free thinking.

3. There is a tendency on the part of some academics to dismiss your fiction as being merely journalistic, dealing with the circles of political power because you, as a member of the Nehru family, have had the insight into the goings on around you. While there is some truth in it, you are largely concerned with depicting the human side of the picture. Have you sufficiently dealt with the middle class and lower middle class officials and politicians? I don't think all the politicians and officials in India can lead the kind of posh life that Devi could lead. Of course, Devi had her Rishad.
4. One of the things that impressed me most about *A Situation in New Delhi* is that while describing your "traditional" subject of politics and personalities, you try to bring out the struggles for "change" in those hierarchies. In short, you are taking pains to portray all the turmoil of revolution or the rumblings of revolution that the Indian life at that level makes evident. What do you think of the opinion of the man on the street, at places like New Delhi, toward what has been happening in the cozy nooks of politicians and officials? You have ignored the average city man.
5. Novels like *A Situation in New Delhi* are technically interesting too. You seem to have managed the psychological technique in the latest novel. The shift from the present to the past and back is managed exquisitely in describing the experiences of Devi, Michael and other characters. While describing Shivraj, you are so nostalgic about your uncle Pandit Nehru! I wonder if, in a future novel, you could portray Madam Indira Gandhi. She is subject for more than a novel. Perhaps you should revise and rewrite *A Situation in New Delhi* in the light of pre- and post-Emergency life in India.

Will you please let me know if you are specifically attracted to any of the psychological novelists or you are just using in your work the flashback technique?

6. What do you think of the political novels in the West?

I will be grateful if you could respond to the points I have raised.

Best Regards,

Sincerely yours,
D. Ramakrishna

* * * * *

New Delhi,
August 5, 1978

Dear Dr. Ramakrishna,

I hope you got my postcard in response to your letter (containing questions) dated July 8th. I now enclose my replies. Your questions are rather large and it has been difficult for me to reply properly to them. Each one would need an essay in reply and I have not had time for this. However, I have done the best I can and I hope my answers will be of some help to you. You may like to see the critique Heinemann have just brought out on my work—part of their series on Indian writers.

I hear that our universities are generally not interested in Indo-English fiction. So I am glad your Department of English is bringing out a journal of English studies.

With best wishes,

Yours sincerely,
Nayantara Sahgal

Answers to Questions

1. There are "average" Indian women at different levels—the rural average, the urban average, and in the rural and urban areas there are again averages at different levels. I do not think there is any such thing as an "average Indian woman." I think change has, in particular, affected the lower middle class, where in the North since partition women have had to get jobs to supplement the family's income. Families that

would never have sent their daughters to college earlier, started to do so because a college degree qualified them for better jobs. So I think there has been a big change towards modernity in this section of society, along with some of the changes in attitudes that working for a living brings. Probably in rural society there has been very little change in a woman's daily round, or attitudes towards her. As far as the character of Devi is concerned, she is already—because of her privileged position and her opportunities—an emancipated woman, and she takes her own emancipation for granted. She is not struggling for it, or under the kind of tensions that a woman from another background might be. She is not having to make difficult choices with regard to personal freedom.

2. I have not tried to expose the hollowness of the "system," as you say, because when I wrote my novels, I believed in the system. I have tried in these novels to show what power does to people. On the other hand (though each novel shows the bad effects of power on certain kinds of personality) I have also shown the "good" men—those who within the same system, work dedicatedly and uncorrupted for what they believe in. The hero of *Storm in Chandigarh*, Vishal Dubey, is an idealistic and upright civil servant. Of the two politicians in the novel, one represents the "power" syndrome, the other does not, so your generalised statement is not correct.
3. This is a very large question and seems to cover a lot of ground. My fiction is certainly not "journalistic" —and I am not even sure what is meant by that. Fiction is about people, basically about character. Nor does every writer have to deal with every class of society and every problem of society. It depends on what he is writing about. My books cover the lower to upper middle class. Devi is an aristocrat—by birth and privilege and opportunity. Naturally all politicians and officials cannot be like her.
4. Again, a novel is concerned with the characters it creates. You will find what you call "the average city man" in *A Time to be Happy* and *This Time of Morning*, as well as in minor

characters like Devi's driver, in Madhu and in Devi's P.A.—at different levels of the city scale—in *A Situation in New Delhi*.

5. No, I would not like to portray Mrs. Gandhi in a novel. At least I cannot imagine doing so just yet. I have recently written a book about her period in power, 1966-77, *Indira Gandhi's Emergence and Style*, which also discusses her personality in one chapter (Published in January by Vikas). No, I am not attracted to the psychological novelists.
6. Some are good, some are bad. Morris West's *Ambassador* is good.

Nayantara Sahgal

Seshendra Sarma

Warangal
July 11, 1978

Dear Sri Seshendra Sarma,

I have today received a copy of Kavi Sena Publication's *Current Scene of Telugu Poetry* posted in Hyderabad. Either you have sent the thing to me or encouraged someone to send it to me. Anyway, I thank you for thinking of me as one of the possible readers of the pamphlet. The contents of the pamphlet echo several of the ideas you so fervently expressed both at the "Ishta Goshti" and personally to me at the Municipal Guest House in Warangal during your trip to this place.

The pamphlet has arrived just on time to be used by me for my review article on Telugu poetry for *The Indian Express*. I will be grateful if you could arrange to send me a copy of *Kavi Sena Manifesto*. You have both the moral and intellectual courage and the necessary resources to launch major intellectual movements like this and I wish you all the best.

I am sorry, I couldn't call on you during my visit to Hyderabad on the 26th of June. I shall, however, be there within a month or two on another visit and then I hope to see you. I will be happy if I could join you on a major intellectual crusade with ramifications both in India and abroad. I have already been doing something with writers like Mulk Raj Anand. By the way, you should read Dr. Anand's major critical work on the Indian novel—from the ancient times upto Prem Chand and Sarat Chandra Chatterjee. He tries to evolve a new myth of the modern Indian consciousness. A few months ago, at the request of Dr. Anand, I had the good fortune of extensively editing the manuscript for publication. He writes that he is preparing the final draft for the press.

Once again, thank you for sending me the pamphlet on Telugu poetry.

With warm regards,

Sincerely yours,
D. Ramakrishna

* * * * *

Hyderabad
July 29, 1978

Dear Sri Ramakrishna,

I was happy to receive your letter after we returned from Warangal. We were looking forward to meeting you here on the 25th/26th of June as your second postcard indicated and were disappointed when you did not come. Therefore the silence in anticipation of hearing from you again. Your recent postcard explains why you could not make it.

Much water has flown under the bridge since we met. I am back in Government service posted as Secretary, Municipal Corporation here. How intricate and intriguing the Government organisation can be! I am now a spoke in the wheel with no option but to move with it.

I am trying to secure a copy of the *Manifesto* which was not readily available as all the copies are handed over to Kavi Sena. They have promised to send me a few copies tomorrow; you shall have your copy soon.

Your comments on the word "Manifesto" and its ideology on aesthetics, its socio-political conceptions may be justified from your point of view. But a party formed for a purpose has its own set of ideals and objectives which necessarily project its own point of view. No individual or an organisation based on a cause can forsake the ethos of its conscience and mould its thinking and action to suit the likes and dislikes of others. A work is an honest expression of the writer's personality. Manifesto is a response to the contemporaneity of my times.

The "red rag" which seems to frighten many people is not really so frightening. The socio-economic theory (concept) represented by Marx has been there from times immemorial as a subconscious urge for justice. Coming down the centuries, gaining in slow but steady intensity ultimately crystallised in the emergence of *Das Capital*. Don't you feel that the modern economists and the 20th century governments have also gradually undergone a change, a modification and approximated themselves to this theory? Is this not a vindication of the "spirit of the age"? Please refer to my preface to *Gorilla*.

Manifesto is an effort made for the first time in the history of aesthetics (in any Indian language) to co-ordinate thought both old and new; and to locate the logical and biological links between art and society. Please read the chapter on "Atma Kala." I would also suggest you to read such of the letters from *In defence of People & Poetry* as referred to on page 253 of *Manifesto* for an accurate understanding of the content of Marxism *as represented by Kavi Sena*.

The language of the *Kavi Sena Manifesto* emerges out of the context of Telugu literature and the present socio-political circumstances. Kavi Sena is a movement born out of the present milieu; therefore it cannot assume the pretentious garb of a mere classroom work. That would render the whole issue a tame domestic affair. Abstruse subjects like aesthetics, poetry, politics and sociology have been explained in the simplest terms possible in the context where they assume indivisible inter-relationship and made into a layman's treat. This I do feel. Of course, there will be different opinions, I shall come in for more attacks for calling a spade a spade, but I am convinced my voice will live beyond it.

My wife and I were very happy to meet you in Warangal. Pity we could not spend more time together. On your next visit to Hyderabad please do not forget to look us up.

My wife joins me in sending you our warm regards,

Yours sincerely,
Seshendra Sarma

* * * * *

Warangal
August 5, 1978

Dear Sri Seshendra Sarma,

Thank you for your letter of July 29 and the copy of *Kavi Sena Manifesto*. I am glad that the small note on a postcard served the purpose for which it was intended (in a Kavi Sena way)—to stimulate you into making your position clearer by means of a copy of the *Manifesto*.

Kindly rest assured that I endorse the central thesis of your work. In a country like ours one cannot ignore the millions living in the rural areas (and in the urban too) under substandard conditions. But the "suffering" is often mitigated by the Indian's innate sense of the Karmic process, a great heritage that makes man on this subcontinent stronger than the Westerner. I say so to my American friends also. Between these two extremes of poverty and philosophy, however, stands the unconcerned middle-class Indian who has enough to eat. The word "unconcerned" may go against the very spirit of Kavi Sena. Of course, this middle-class citizen has his own peculiar problems. He cannot be classified a "worker" in the Marxist sense. Hence, I'm afraid your "Fraternity of Writers and Workers" with the symbol of a sickle, does not represent the totality of the Indian experience, even though the whole thing sounds okay (for publicity reasons) to make your *Manifesto* "click." I'm sure it will click, but needs slight modifications.

With warm regards,

Yours sincerely,
D. Ramakrishna

* * * * *

Warangal
August 18, 1978

Dear Sri Seshendra Sarma,

Thank you for your goodwill in sending me a copy of *Samudram Naa Peru*. I have quite enjoyed reading it. Not only the title but the contents too unfold before the reader the profound depths and vastness of your being—like the sea itself. While on the one hand you take the reader with you on a journey into your innermost self, on the other you show him the expansive universe around—a universe that does not exclude life on earth. Reading a poem like this together with another like *Gorilla* shows the two facets of your personality—the sublunary and the subterranean! You had told the meeting held at the Town Hall here last summer that the Emergency excesses occasioned the writing of *Gorilla*. The human side of the issue is quite sad in the particular context; but the universalizing of such an experience is perhaps more than the reader can swallow. Both in intellectual content and in the get-up, the present publication (*Samudram Naa Peru*) is more admirable than the earlier work. You may say I can say anything I like and that you won't mind my saying so!

Nevertheless, I trust that you appreciate my unflattering views on your work from time to time.

With warm regards,

Sincerely,
D. Ramakrishna

* * * * *

Hyderabad
August 27, 1978

Dear Shri Ramakrishna,

Thank you for your letter, received on my return from Tirupati yesterday.

I am glad you liked *Sumudram Naa Peru*. As you correctly said it is another facet of my mind. I do not think a poet should be restricted. But thinking and writing is another matter. . . .

Let me assure you I value your opinion whether flattering or unflattering because it emanates from an honest person.

With kind regards,

Yours sincerely,
Seshendra Sarma

* * * * *

Warangal
August 28, 1978

Dear Mrs. Indira Devi,

I have read with interest a brief sketch on you, Sri Sarma and the Pakistani poet Faiz by Sri G. Krishna in *The Sunday Standard*. Some of the remarks made by the writer may be worth scrutiny in the light of your actual work. You had earlier sent me your recent collection entitled *Poems of My National Conscious-*

ness (this title will be better than the one you had given!). The word "memory" sounds odd. Would you please send me copies of the other five or six collections of your poetry to enable me to understand the recent collection better? If fact, last summer you told me that you would send me your other works too. But you didn't.

Sri Seshendra Sarma might be lost in the labyrinths of the Hyderabad Municipal Corporation. God save him! I look forward to hearing from you.

By the way, Dr. Mulk Raj Anand writes to me that he would be in Hyderabad in January. He may then make a trip to Warangal too on an assignment by the Lalit Kala Akademi to work on Kakatiya Art and Sculpture. He wants me to undertake the second and final round of editing of his 300-page manuscript on the Indian novel. I like the young old man and love the labour of editing his work too.

Please give my regards to Sri Seshendra Sarma.

Best Regards,

Yours Sincerely,
D. Ramakrishna

* * * * *

Hyderabad
20 September, 1978

Dear Sri Ramakrishna,

We ought to have written to you after returning from Warangal first but events caught us in their grip soon after our return. . . . I had to postpone all my writing and correspondence which I very much regret. Meeting you at Warangal was a happy surprise. In fact you were a different person than your outspoken letters through which I had tried to picture you earlier. Therefore meeting you was rewarding. To judge you without meeting would be an injustice. You are no more Indo-Anglian than I am; your roots are too deep in Indian literature even though you may teach English. This is one thing about you; you must not change like others who have lost their identity and are trying to recapture it again in a vain hope. Once the personality breaks, no one can put it together.

Thank you for your letter. The article in *The Indian Express* surprised me a little, for that is not all what I had said. In fact, he left out the importance of Faiz Ahmed Faiz in the context of Urdu literature. I tried to tell him this but obviously it was beyond his grasp. There is a lovely picture of Faiz and Seshendra in the *Andhra Prabha* weekly.

Separately I have mailed two books to you. Those are the only ones I have. My earlier works are out of print. Since 1970 I have relegated myself and my writing in favour of Seshendra. I had taken up his fight. We had steep odds against which we had to work. During that time I began keeping a journal and now from these pages I have worked out my autobiography called *The Tree of My Womanhood*. It should go to print sometime this year. I shall have it retyped and send it for your opinion. My latest volume of poems *Wind Blows from the Scaffold* will be out next month with a little bit of luck. If you are interested I shall let you have a typed copy. You would have preferred the name of my last book to have been *Poems of my National Conscience*; yet I still think "memory" is more apt, more poetic, *Partings in Mimosa* was the last tame poem I wrote . . . it was incidentally put up by 17 countries or rather nominated by 17 countries for the Nobel in 1973/74. I do not remember correctly. That is because I do not write for recognition by awards . . . writing for me is a process of evolving on many planes of life.

Enough of myself. Trust this finds you well. Look forward to hearing from you,

With warm regards,

Yours sincerely,
Indira Devi Dhanrajgir

* * * * *

Hyderabad (New Delhi)
November 6, 1978

Dear Shri Ramakrishna,

Got your letter before leaving. It will be a good idea to meet Mulk Raj Anand here at our place provided we could have the dates in advance.

Regards,

Sincerely,
Indira Devi Dhanrajgir

* * * * *

Hyderabad
December 1, 1978

Dear Shri Ramakrishna,

Received your kind letter. I received "Vimarshini," read the review and wrote to Shri Shastri. He has brilliant critical acumen.

About your suggestion to "bring out a series of critical studies on various forms of Telugu writing in English language," I think it is a very complicated project for a man like me. You know my views on current Telugu literature. Then how to proceed with it. We shall discuss the matter in detail when we meet.

Yours sincerely,
Seshendra Sarma

* * * * *

Warangal
December 3, 1978

Dear Mrs. Indira Devi,

Thank you for the telegram telling me about Dr. Anand's visit to your place on the sixth of December. Yesterday I sent a telegram to you in reply. I will be there at your place reaching Hyderabad by the Golconda Express. I would like to use the trip to bring Dr. Anand here to Warangal. We are arranging a lecture by him here on the 7th evening. On the 8th, Dr. Anand will be able to go to Ramappa for his study of Kakatiya art. I have suggested to Dr. Anand that he should take the guidance of Sri D. Someswara Rao, who has specialized in the subject and written for the Andhra Pradesh Lalit Kala Akademi.

I look forward to seeing you and Sri Sarma there on the 6th.

Regards,

Yours sincerely,
D. Ramakrishna

* * * * *

Ootakamund
June 12, 1979

My dear Ramakrishna,

Sorry for the delay in writing to you. I am really glad that my talk could please such an accomplished critic and aesthetician like you, to whose opinions I attach considerable value.

I believe that all the great achievements of man in the realm of knowledge have an imperceptible mutual relation and in their totality only have a profound significance and relevance to the progress of mankind. Though apparently conflicting, most of the intellectual theories blend into the over-all homogeneity implicit in the wider structure of cognition of reality. I found this generally underlying all systems of knowledge, like for instance, I found it in the Indian poetics. Vakrokti, Dhwani, Chamatkara, though propounded as separate theories, essentially represent the same principle underlying all poetry. The various systems of philosophy in any part of the world similarly grope to reach one and the same reality, their conflicts being only surfacial. It was Leelashuka who presented this truth in the most profound terms possible. From Socrates to Marx the distance may be too far but it is circular and not linear. The distance between Sri Chakra and Marx also is similarly apparent and one of modality. Marx's dialectical materialism traces the origin of creation to matter, and Sri Chakra whose primary concern is exponence of the principle of creation, also lays emphasis on the crucial role of matter in the creative process. Matter in Prakriti which means Shakti. The first Sutra of the Shankara's *Soundaryalahari* lays down that Purusha is incapable of action in the absence of Shakti. This is all of course understandable only at the metaphysical levels of these theories. At the physical level they are riddled with vulgarized antagonisms all of which are only accretions of the ignorance of blind folks in politics and literature. But the visionary mind always revels in discovering the integrity of the whole in life and cognition of life.

You see now how you stimulated my mind into thinking so far and so deep that I left the common level of a friendly letter.

Trust you are well. We will be in Hyderabad by the 18th. Do write there.

Warm regards,

Yours sincerely,
Seshendra Sarma

* * * * *

Hyderabad
December 14, 1980

My Dear Ramakrishna,

I received your affectionate letter which reminded me of your simple and unassuming person laden with the glow of love for art and literature. It is a long time that I met you. Had you telephoned to me when you were here I could have arranged for your being fetched here. However, do not miss the opportunity of meeting us next time when you are in Hyderabad. Just ring me up, I shall arrange to send the car.

Yours sincerely,
Seshendra Sarma

* * * * *

Warangal
January 31, 1981

Dear Sri Seshendra Sarma,

I've just received *Premalekhalu, Seshendra Kavitha* which you have so kindly sent me, and eagerly read it to discover more about the man and poet in you. Even though the languages in which we are functioning are different, the commonness of our mother tongue and culture has indeed endeared me to your mind. *Premalekhalu*, as the translator Sri Nirmal puts it, is something unique in Indian literature. Unlike the statements of poets like Kamala Das in Indian-English poetry, there is in your book urbanity and aristocracy of taste. Whether overtly stated or just hinted at, most of what goes on for love poetry by our distinguished writers in English is downright sexual perversion which they try to pass off as "authentic" experience. One should read a book like yours in order to know about the inner workings of the mind of a love poet. Your great relationship with Smt. Indira Devi reminds one of what happened between Robert Browning and Elizabeth Barrett. These letters and any other literary dialogue between you and Mrs. Indira Devi will have a place in

Telugu love poetry as much as the correspondence of Robert and Elizabeth Browning in the nineteenth-century English poetry.

The other day I had received the postcard from Mrs. Indira Devi. Please give my regards to her. By the way, I will be at the American Studies Research Centre in Hyderabad during the whole of the first week of March, continuing the revision of my Ph.D. thesis on Poe's tales for publication in book form. Last year I was already there three times. They have extended the grant into this year too. In the first week of March, thus, I will surely go to your place.

My first book *Indian-English Prose: An Anthology* (Arnold-Heinemann, 1980) has been reviewed well in *The Hindustan Times*, *Amrita Bazar Patrika*, *Hitavada*, *Cygnus*, *World Literature Today*, etc. More reviews are expected during the next few months. This seems to have proved a good beginning for my book-publishing career. It's a pity, however, I have yet to complete the first book of my creative writing in English (Prose). Instead of ending up as a critic, I should do some original writing. I see the distant glimmerings of that.

With warm regards,

Yours sincerely,
D. Ramakrishna

* * * * *

Warangal
April 18, 1981

Dear Sri Seshendra Sarma,

Mrs. Indira Devi might have told you about my phone call on the 6th of April. After an 8-day spell of work at the American Studies Research Centre, I returned to Warangal on the 13th.

I have just received *Vedana Sikharalu* by Samad and leaflet from Kharagpur, both obviously mailed to me at your suggestion. Thank you. Kavi Sena is indeed emerging into a major literary movement. I suggest that you think of making it more popular through the medium of English language. Serious students of Indian English literature too could be made to take interest in the publications of your organization. Since literature in translation is gaining currency in Indian and Western Universities, you should evolve a more ambitious global strategy to popularize Kavi Sena.

I'm indeed sorry I missed you during my stay in Hyderabad. The very fact that you are one of the official delegates to the Malaysia conference proves that you are no longer at war with the government. I know that you are different from the sycophants heard over the All India Radio, Hyderabad. In fact, in the course of one of my visits to you (a couple of years ago) I was suggesting that you should tone down your voice against the Establishment. Of course, I never mean to under-estimate your individuality and self-respect as a writer. But what I meant was depending upon the way of the world, the wise man should slightly alter his strategy for survival, literary or otherwise.

Are you likely to be in Hyderabad in May?

Please give my regards to Mrs. Indira Devi.

Yours sincerely,
D. Ramakrishna

* * * * *

Hyderabad
January 21, 1983

My Dear Dr. Ramakrishna,

Thank you very much for your book *Indian English Prose*, which I shall read in due course and write to you.

Your letter was received after you returned to Warangal. It was nice meeting you after such ages. Look forward to seeing you in Hyderabad soon.

With our warm regards,

Yours sincerely,
Indira Devi Dhanrajgir

* * * * *

Hyderabad
February 1, 1983

My Dear Dr. Ramakrishna,

We have been trying to get seats for Attenborough's *Gandhi*. I am sure it is a great film. No doubt it must have moved a person as sensitive as Dr. Mulk Raj Anand and filled him with nostalgia. My father took me to see Gandhiji when he was detained in the Agha Khan palace at Poona. Dr. Roy and Sarojini Naidu were staying with us. I met Gandhiji twice, once when I was a child and once after the independence. So you know Dr. K.V.S. Murthy of Andhra University. Yes, I have read some of his poems. If writing articles on poets gives you satisfaction, can I send you my latest poem "The Wind blows from the Scaffold" and request you to write?

Do let us know when you are coming next to Hyderabad, so that we can spend an evening together.

Seshandra joins me in sending you our fond regards,

Yours sincerely,
Indira Devi Dhanrajgir

* * * * *

Warangal
February 3, 1983

Dear Mrs. Indira Devi,

Thank you for your letter of February 1. I've gradually entered the climate of American studies research-work on the two books. And I should be out of it by the end of summer this year. The Director of the ASRC (Prof. Robert Crunden) told me that he would give a fresh research grant in a few weeks so I could spend the summer in Hyderabad. In the meantime, of course, I may have to go there at least once. I think during my summer trip I can call on you again.

Please do send me your works including the latest. Even though I'm really no specialist in Indian Writing in English, I will try to explicate your work. In July last, while at Bombay University as Ph.D. examiner, after the viva I had to tell the supervisor of the candidate privately that I was not really a "specialist"! But then they said I had published a book and several papers on Indian Writing in English. Nevertheless I still feel I'm basically an "Americanist," and there is no exaggeration in this confession.

If you still feel I can write on your work, please do send your works to me. But I can start reading them only after June/July this year. I suffer from no complexes or scruples in writing about friendly writers in an unflattering manner. We are living in a world and times when sheer sycophancy or malicious denigration will be the order of the day. I avoid both.

With warm regards to you & Seshendra,

Sincerely,
D. Ramakrishna

* * * * *

Hyderabad
July 6, 1983

My dear Ramakrishna,

I really enjoyed your enlightened company the other day at Gyanbagh.

I got the "Interview" typed out again. (Portions of it were read over to you) I am now sending herewith the copy for favour of your introduction.

With your introduction it will be published as soon as the introduction is received.

With kind regards,

Yours sincerely,
Seshendra Sarma

* * * * *

Hyderabad
July 14, 1983

Dear Ramakrishna,

I received your inland cover and today's card. I thank you very much for the interest you have taken about my son. Can't you write to your friend in New York before your father-in-law leaves for the place? See if it is possible.

I am glad you received the "Interview." I hope you will let me know your views.

Thanking you,

Yours sincerely,
Seshendra Sarma

* * * * *

Warangal
September 6, 1983

Dear Sri Seshendra Sarma,

There has been some delay in completing my own work and commenting on yours on account of another labour of love—commenting on the MS of a novel in English (*The Unvanquished*) done by a college lecturer at Mancherial. His friends collected ten thousand rupees to publish the novel and the printer has been ready to start composing. Even though I did not know the author before June this year, I couldn't turn down his request for comments on account of my own interest in creative writing. I advised him to get in touch with Dr. Mulk Raj Anand for a "Foreword," but Dr. Anand asked him to get it from me. Hence I shall compose that too. The book is the author's first effort in novel writing, even though his short stories appeared earlier in *The Hindu*. He will send a copy to you also. Kindly speak about the work to your friends in Hyderabad and elsewhere. The author, Sri Sudhakar Rao, is a good man and deserves every encouragement.

Yours sincerely,
D. Ramakrishna

* * * * *

Hyderabad
October 11, 1983

My dear Dr. Ramakrishna,

I received the manuscript (*My Country, My People*) yesterday. Thank you very much for taking such keen interest and going through the pages so diligently. Your valuable suggestions will go a long way in making the book more comely. You will be glad to learn that the book has gone to the press.

Warm regards,

Yours sincerely,
Seshendra Sarma

* * * * *

Bombay
November 12, 1983

Dear Dr. Ramakrishna,

I was thinking of writing to you as soon as I reached Delhi, but due to the hectic atmosphere in which I was involved ever since I reached there, I could not write. I reached here a few days ago and found myself in a comparatively quieter surroundings.

It is a pity we could not meet in Hyderabad. We left for Delhi soon after I received your letter. I asked Vanamali to see you if possible, but I do not know whether he would, because he was in a hurry to leave for Nellore.

I think I informed you that the "Interview" went to the press with your corrections. Its progress is however held up due to our leaving Hyderabad. We will resume it seen after we return.

Trust this finds you well,

Yours sincerely,
Seshendra Sarma

* * * * *

Hyderabad
November 28, 1983

Dear Shri Ramakrishna,

Receiving your letter was like looking at a garden sparkling in the early rays of sun on a winter day. It was so refreshing in this murky atmosphere of wretched Telugu literature in the city. Hope you will not miss meeting us during your next visit.

Yours sincerely,
Seshendra Sarma

* * * * *

Hyderabad
December 1, 1983

Dear Dr. Ramakrishna,

I received your letter and was really shocked to know of the incident.

My wife and myself convey to you our deep concern for your welfare. We will do all that we can in the matter.

More in due course.

Yours most sincerely,
Seshendra Sarma

* * * * *

Hyderabad
March 2, 1984

My dear Ramakrishna,

I received your letter 27/2. I have no contact with Mr. Nissim Ezekiel. In fact, I have hardly any contact in the Indo-Anglian field except friends like you. But most of them have a narrow or rather limited view of literature and therefore think I belong to an outside language and so literature wise I am a "foreigner." However, I value their friendship, as I believe human relations are more valuable than superficial relations in the name of literature. Why don't you kindly translate a few of those poster poems if you find time? That would lend some authenticity and also colour besides credibility in the eyes of Shri Ezekiel. But the main Anthology of poems of Kavi Sena, called *Kommalu Cheelchukuni Vastayee Poolu* is most important. It was mailed to you early last year.

Looking forward to seeing you in Hyderabad,

With warm regards,

Yours sincerely,
Seshendra Sarma

* * * * *

Hyderabad
July 18, 1984

My dear Dr. Ramakrishna,

Your visit to Gyan Bagh last week with the "Grail Book" (*From Ritual to Romance* by Jessie Weston. T.S. Eliot used the book while writing of *The Waste Land*) has not been a mere visit in my eyes; but in the context of the work in which I am involved at present it is a mystery in the real occult sense of the term. This receives emphasis by the object of the visit being to seek illumination on the subject from me. Your visit when it was scheduled was only the hazy picture of a casual event without any special significance before its occurrence; but now it is an event with an inscrutable meaning and baffling any attempts at ratiocination.

During your stay I gave you in the course of our dialogue a sketchy account of my involvement in a folklore tale of which I had to speak at the Andhra Saraswathi Parishad on 3rd June 1984 as an introduction to the volume of Dr. T.V. Subba Rao of Bangalore University on his doctoral thesis on Janapada. I told you that the story of Ankamma, a village deity, included in the volume was pregnant with tremendous possibilities of being the provenance of the "time concept in Rig-Veda" and its derivative form of the Uttanka tale of the *Mahabharata*. Though I mentioned meagre material when relating it to you due to the physical and mental exhaustion I was passing through at that time, I gave a fairly cogent picture of my theory in my speech, that Ankamma story is the original form of Rg-Vedic symbols of yarn and the spinning wheel and that Vyasa had heavily drawn from Rig-Veda and the Ankamma legend. The theory included millenniums of time duration, conception and growth of symbols and myth in the womb of racial time, clash and synthesis of cults and cultures and a million other subtle things that raised their head in the ferment of such a style of thinking. I am recalling this to your mind only to help you apprehend the significance of what I said of your visit. This is only to say that I was already in the bewildering maze of thought, reason, imagination, intuition and instinct and a hundred other tentacles of the octopus of my mind. In this connection the Grail book comes to me from almost the fingers of the last century and the voice of the author reaches me like signals from yonder star; above all, your carrying it to Gyan Bagh launching on an intended journey whose avowed object of a dialogue with me was as I said a mystery which is only to be felt but defies reasoning.

From Ritual to Romance is a monument of quest and scholarship and a study of it impresses the reader unmistakably that it is well based on the dialectics of Mythology evolved in the modern systems of knowledge about symbols, myths, and occult mysteries. It offers a rich fare of exciting reading and countless thrills of brilliant-minded research. No wonder if the great poet of our century T.S. Eliot was inspired by this work to write his magnum opus *The Waste Land*. We admire chiefly the rare vision of the author which, penetrating into the hoary past, captures the original source or sources of the Grail legend now found embedded in Christian liturgy.

Though her reference to Indra freeing waters, to Thammuz and Adonis for the concept of death and resurrection, then to the sword dances of Maruts and others, to the English Mumming plays near Rugby in England, are relevant to her investigation, they do not solve the Grail problem and they are separate, not forming integral parts of the organic ensemble of a single story, which was in fact her complaint against the other scholars working on the subject.

The author points out many variations in the character and incidents in the different versions of Bowain, Percival, Peredur, Diu Crone, Perlesvaus, Sone de Nansai, Parsival and others; and it is quite natural that a legend of such vitality as the Grail one being the product of a raw primitive society millenniums ago, is bound to spread across different peoples of different races over different ages and give rise to numerous variants in the structure, as well as in the elements of the legend. The author settling one of these versions as the earliest and then proceeding to examine the later variants and also on that basis attributing the soil of the story to the British Isles does not appear to be plausible. She should have, I think, consulted other versions earlier than Chrestean De Troies and some later Old English versions. For instance, (1) Mabinogion (Welsh Stories) MSS dated 14th century; (2) Red Book; (3) Kulhwich and the Dream of Ronabury; (4) Historia Britonum by Nennius—9th century; (5) Book of Geoffrey of Monmouth—1152 AD; (6) Morte d' Arthur by Malory; (7) the Misfortunes of Arthur by Thomas Hughes' play 1588 AD (enacted before the queen), (8) Dryden's opera on King Arthur or The British Worthy; (9) Layamon a priest of Arley Regis, supposed to be the first poet to sing of Arthur in English verse. He is said to have lived in the 13th century. From the plethora of material that she had strewn over her pages, it looks as though the story either emerged in some of the regions of Asia Minor or broadly speaking, made a journey from the East towards the West. Among the so many variants that the author introduced to us in the book, the nearest and the fullest counterpart is only the episode of "Rishyashringa" of the *Mahabharata*. The real mistake has arisen only here and thereby compelled her to wade through a morass of enormous legendary material of all the regions covering from Asia to Europe. I think, had she taken the

Rishyashringa version of the *Ramayana* instead of the one of the *Mahabharata*, she would have had on her hands such a complete and perfect version of the picture of the Grail legend that all the puzzling questions that kept on raising demanding answers all the way through her work would not have arisen at all, because the version of the *Ramayana* has all the answers to all the questions that arose due to the mutilated shapes and variants that she had with her. The *Ramayana* version actually contains the element of "quest" "wasteland," the "rain" "two kings" one of whom was the cause of wasteland, the principle of fertility, the Grail and the lance. These are the essential elements which require research and solution in the Grail legend and they are all available in the *Ramayana* version. The solution lies there in the form of an actual ritual of fertility. The *Ramayana* episode actually describes the most ancient ritual coming down from ages of hoary past to its own times. The ritual is two-fold—the first part Asvamedha and the other Putreshti. The first is Vedic ritual and the second Tantric drawn from Atharva siroh mantras which were a conglomeration of native hymns; not yet grafted into Vedas to form the fourth Veda. The lance is in the first part where the queen desirous of pregnancy stays with the sacred horse for one complete night; it obviously indicates that the bovine penis is the lance and in the second part of the ritual, a divine figure called "prajapathya purusha" comes out of the sacrificial fire holding a cup (patra) of "ksheera" which has power to impregnate the queens of Dasaratha. This is the Grail. (It may be noted here that these rituals are described in the *Ramayana* and not in the *Mahabharata*. It may also be noted that whereas in the *Ramayana* Aswamedha is a fertility ritual, in the *Mahabharata* it is a ritual of military invasion of a king for imperial expansion.)

Jessie L. Weston herself based her research on the presumption that the lance and Grail are the genitals of male and female but she could not show anywhere a legendary instance where the lance was identified with the phallus. When I point out that the bovine phallus is the lance in the Ramayanic ritual, the idea is that the phallus itself is a symbol. However, we may also shift the symbolic role from the actual phallus of the horse to the three swords with which the queen touches the horse at certain places/points in the course of the horse ritual. I have also noted Will Durant mentioning in his *Story of Civilisation* that the phallus was engraved on the walls of Egyptian temples as a cross with handle as a sign of sexual union and vigorous life (Crux ansata, p.199).This I consider is of great value in the context of this work because lance representing male genitals in the Grail legend could be directly traced to ancient Egyptian symbolism.

Reading *From Ritual to Romance* I was reminded of the Grail subject which I read years ago in Will Durant's *Story of Civilisation*. However, I didn't realise all the significance of the legend until I read it in the pages of Jessie Weston.

Her references to Rudra as a deity of departed souls and her drawing correspondence between Apsaras and Gandharvas and the Greek Nymphs and Satyrs are not satisfactory. The statement that the Gandharvas are spirits of fertility of a lower order, is obviously not correct. To describe Shiva as an ethonian deity perhaps merely based on the fact of the "Indian Practice" of making Shiva Lingas with earth may not be a concept sound enough. Next, the sword dance of Maruts is also rather far-fetched. The chapters of the Fisher King and the Medicine Man, though full of apparent relevance, do not actually satisfy as happy and convincing chapters. Her statement on page 108 that Gawain's character of healer belongs to him in his role of Grail Winner, contradicts with the theories advanced in the other pages. I cannot go into details.

Discussing about Adonis as the fertility God the writer tells us that he died out of a wound in the thigh caused by a wild boar and due to the wailings and prayers of Aphrodite, his beloved, he had been permitted by Zeus to come back to life on earth for sometime to be with Persephone. When Adonis is in Hades, the earth becomes "wasteland" . . . and when he returns, earth is restored to life with vegetation and water. But as far as I know of Greek mythology, this role which is assigned to Adonis here in fact belongs to Persephone who is the goddess of Spring forcibly carried away by the God of Hades and married. Due to the wrath and sorrow of her mother Demeter, earth was rendered waste and

Zeus interferes and arranges that Persephone be permitted to return and stay with her mother Demeter for sometime and go back and remain in Hades for sometime. When Persephone is in Hades, earth turns into a desert land and when she returns to earth to join her mother, life, water and vegetation are restored to earth, with Spring and singing birds. Perhaps I do not know enough of Greek mythology to reconcile this variation.

References to fish in the Buddhistic religion on page 126 and the statement on page 127 that both in India and China fish is employed in funeral rites, are unsavoury observations, hastily made without verification.

The author kept on shifting the underlying principles of the legend from one to the other. In the first place the underlying principle was, to start with, a journey of quest and releasing of waters to cure lifeless earth. As the book progresses further the underlying principle becomes death and resurrection, mourning and rejoicing and finally the underlying principle changes to fertility. Since the structure of the work does not appeal to the reader as homogeneous, though he is deeply impressed with the material and the argument, the ultimate meaning of the work does not emerge as an organic whole but looks like dismembered limbs strewn over. It is this feeling that leads to the shifting sense regarding the underlying principle of the legend. In fact, the intelligent and informed reader will however realize that all the three variations of the underlying principle mentioned above have an essential unity that is in the principle of fertility and that the Grail legend is a symbolic representation of perhaps a fertility ritual emanating from the visions of a primitive society.

Reading the author's treatment of the aspect of death and resurrection found in the episode of Adonis, I was wondering why she missed the legend of Kaama Dahana of Indian mythology. Kamadeva is put to death and later revived to life. His death was vanishing of all that was beautiful in creation and his resurrection was the return of Spring. This episode fits so correctly into the context as Rishyashringa of the *Ramayana* fits in the context of quest and rain.

All this is a critical appreciation of Jessie L.Weston's *From Ritual to Romance*. As you close the book and recline into a mood of retrospection you cannot help admiring the great value of the work. We admire her for her deep insight, profound awareness of the unity of human mind and its legend and her scholarship, above all her vision which makes great adventures into the hazardous realms of the illusive mysteries of occult symbols, the Grail, the lance, the Fisher King and so on. She has a passion for quest tempered with a great conviction. She is neither a casual writer nor a drab academician. We can see all this and more in her pages and especially in the following sentences on pages 186, 187:

1) "Other world is not a myth but a reality, and in all ages there have been souls who have been willing to brave the great adventure and to risk all for the chance of bringing back with them some assurance of the future life."
2) "The truth may lie very deep down, but is there, and it is worth seeking, and Celtic fairy tales, charming as they are, can never afford a satisfactory or an abiding resting place. I for one utterly refuse to accept such as an adequate goal for a life's research. A path that leads but into Celtic Twilight can only be a by-path, and not the King's Highway!"
3) "The Grail Romances repose eventually not upon a poet's imagination, but upon the ruins of an august and ancient ritual, a ritual which once claimed to be the accredited guardian of the deepest secrets of life."

Her passionate voice will ring in our ears for days on end like an oracle, after you close the book.

We shall discuss more when we meet next. Trust this finds you well.

Yours most sincerely,
Seshendra Sarma

* * * * *

Hyderabad
October 1, 1984

Dear Dr. Ramakrishna,

Yours of the 25th Septemebr arrived yesterday, addressed to Seshendra. We are so sorry we retained your book *From Ritual to Romance* which has to be returned to ASRC. Due to unavoidable reasons our meeting has been postponed. Things are becoming better now. Let us hope that October will be peaceful. Some people are interested in shooting a Film at Gyan Bagh between 20th and 31st October which we have not yet decided.

Shall write to you soon or intimate on telephone the best time for you to come. Please advise us what we should do with your book. Would you like us to send it to the library on your behalf? I would not risk posting it to Warangal in case it gets lost. Seshendra and I send our affectionate Dassera and Deepawali greetings to you and your family.

Yours sincerely,
Indira Devi Dhanrajgir

* * * * *

Hyderabad
May 2, 1985

Dear Ramakrishna,

Your letter of February 15.

Your remarks about Viswanatha's programmes there are quite justified. Poor old soul! His literature has no political motives, much less any such colours either. Our friends nowadays on this side or that side cannot approach literature without dabbing some colour or other to it and without smearing the face of the poet with their own rubbish. We are exposed to this political cholera on all sides and pure human feeling has become a smaller value in the hands of these managers of literature. The urgent and the foremost need of the hour in our country and mainly in Telugu-speaking areas is strong measures of disinfecting literature and saving it from the political germs. I am not disdaining politics which is a necessary instrument in achieving peoples' rights in a democracy; but I do disdain that politics which invades into literature. There is a sharp distinction between the two types. While I admit the right of the political parties to exist in a modern society as inevitable forces to save the common man from the degradations of the state, I do question the activities of that tribe of people who wear literary masks and assume the power of determining the fate of poets and writers in literature.

Trust this finds you well.

Yours sincerely,
Seshendra Sarma

* * * * *

Hyderabad
September 20, 1985

Dear Shri Ramakrishna,

About the "Doctorate," I assure you I was not at all annoyed. You did not say anything which could be the cause of annoyance, by any stretch of imagination. This "Doctorate" is complete news to me from the beginning to the present day. There must be some politics in this; only I am a pawn in it without my knowledge. You are acquainted with my literature from which you can guess what value I attach to such matters. But incidentally my regard for Shri Venkatasubbaiah goes up because he never even mentioned this to me. And my acquaintance with him is nominal and also 3 or 4 months old! Naturally I should think that persons like him are rare in the tribe of politicians. I am glad you are visiting Gyan Bagh during your trip to Hyderabad. We will spend some time together discussing your intellectual pursuits. The need for Guru's initiation for sishya (Deeksha) is a tantric concept and needs elaborate explanation.

Yours sincerely,
Seshendra Sarma

* * * * *

Hyderabad
September 23, 1985

My dear Dr. Ramakrishna,

We are well. Sunanda P. Chavan's book *The Fair Voice* on women poets writing in English has been brought out by Sterling Publishers Private Limited, L-10 Green Park Extension, New Delhi—110 016. There is mention about your article also in the Bibliography.

Regarding the Bihar controversy I assure you we are innocent. If Shri Venkatasubbaiah has gone all out to propose our names it shows that he is primarily a good person and has respect for literature.

Seshendra joins me in sending our warm regards to you both.

Yours sincerely,
Indira Devi Dhanrajgir

* * * * *

Hyderabad
May 20, 1986

Dear Shri Ramakrishna,

I am most grateful to you for your kind letter which I received today.

All my efforts at fighting the wrong values of the Telugu literature field have nearly failed and today I stand lonely and frustrated, leaving in the end everything to the sweeping tide of the time.

Thanking you,

Yours sincerely,
Seshendra Sarma

* * * * *

Hyderabad
June 4, 1988

Dear Dr. Ramakrishna,

Thank you very much for your words of sympathy in our tragic hour at the passing away of our beloved father Raja Dhanrajgiriji Bahadur.

Received the manuscript (*My Country, My People*) yesterday after further editing. How shall I thank you for the interest you have bestowed on it? It will take me a few days to come out of the present circumstances. I shall write to you later in more detail.

Warm regards from self and the family to you both.

Yours sincerely,
Rajkumari Saheba Indira Devi

* * * * *

Hyderabad
August 27, 1986

Dear Dr. Ramakrishna,

Received your letter 18/8. I sent "The Book" a couple of days ago, with Dr. P. Jagannadham of your University. I hope you received it by now. It is collected works of my poetry with three new additions. The total work was restructured and issued in a new form, because I decided not to write poetry any longer steeped in this Telugu slush.

Yours sincerely,
Seshendra Sarma

* * * * *

Hyderabad
October 29, 1986

Dear Ramakrishna,

I beg your pardon for the delay in writing reply. I have no idea of the influence of Poe in Telugu. Poe is too different a star for our poets to voyage, I think. Since the process of my poetry was directly under the impact of the blizzards of life, it has not taken any extraneous influence into its fold. My symbols were products of my literary experience.

Yours sincerely,
Seshendra Sarma

* * * * *

Hyderabad
May 21, 1987

Dear Dr. Ramakrishna,

We plan to leave for Greece in June. Seshendra has been invited by the European Centre of Culture in Delphi to participate in the Delphic Festival where he will present a paper on Ancient Greek and Indian Drama. He has not started writing it yet. He is finishing the last pages of his forthcoming novel called *Kaamautsava* in *Andhra Jyoti Weekly*.

While we are away I shall be grateful if you would go through the English translation of Seshendra's poetry. I am sending the xeroxed copies under separate cover. I shall also appreciate if you would correspond with Sterling Publishers or any other (in consultation with Prof. Ezekiel) as you are the Editor of the book. You will be happy to know that *My Country, My People* has been translated into Greek and has received acclaim. We are going to meet the poet who has translated the work in Greece.

You will be hearing from me or rather us soon. In the meantime kindly acknowledge the letter.

With our personal regards to you both.

Yours sincerely,
Indira Devi Dhanrajgir

* * * * *

Hyderabad
October 6, 1987

My dear Dr. Ramakrishna,

We had a glorious trip to Greece and thought of you very often there. Ever since our return I have been meaning to write but we suddenly discovered that I had very high blood pressure. So for nearly two months now I have had to abandon all activities. I am a bit better now.

You are welcome to come and stay with us any time from 25th October to 10th of November. In the third week of November my friend Anna Devari from Greece will be coming and we hope we will be able to stage *Vikramorvasiyam* in January 1988.

Trust this finds you both well. Do drop us a line.

Wish you all a happy Dassera.

Yours sincerely,
Indira Devi Dhanrajgir

P.S.: Are you following Seshendra's novel which is being serialised in *Andhra Jyothi Weekly* called *Kaamautsava*?

* * * * *

Hyderabad
August 18, 1988

Dear Dr. Ramakrishna,

I received your kind letter together with one enclosure. Your account of the Indian literary scene is a disarming exposure of the many opportunistic and misleading agencies that are operating within India.

I am really grateful to you for all the interest that you are taking to advance the cause of my work in literature. Publication of the English versions of my poems naturally involves financial matters. I have to start inducing my wife into it. I shall start the process and let us see.

With kind regards,

Yours sincerely,
Seshendra Sarma

* * * * *

Hyderabad
October 14, 1988

Dear Dr. Ramakrishna,

I was happy to receive your letter dated 11.10.1988. I am really glad that you are visiting America and are going to enjoy the freshness and breeze of America's literary milieu first hand. Such a thing does aid one's awareness of the magnetic touch of reality.

Why don't you think of Indira for inclusion in the literary criticism of Indo-Anglian poetry? Perhaps she is one of the earliest of the poets in India. Hoping to see you in Hyderabad.

Yours sincerely,
Seshendra Sarma

* * * * *

Hyderabad
December 2, 1988

Dear Ramakrishna,

I received your kind letter dated 1.12.1988. I am really glad that my poems appeared in *Indian PEN* and feel grateful to you for all the trouble you have taken in this connection. Hoping to see you in Hyderabad soon.

Yours sincerely,
Seshendra Sarma

* * * * *

Bombay
September 18, 1989

My dear Dr. Ramakrishna,

I received your letter dated 29th August 1989. Due to certain unavoidable preoccupations this delay in writing to you for which you will pardon me. There was also a second thought for a moment whether your letter calls for another from me. . . . In such an indecisive condition of mind I am writing this to you.

Perhaps your friends consider me inferior to what I was formerly, maybe correct, or may not be, because there are other sections of my readers as well who consider the matter the other way about. But my own understanding is that the world is after all an odd assortment of varied opinions and modes of apprehension. And in this confusion which is called the world our concern should be in the art of literature, whether a piece of writing is genuine or not, in other words, whether it is the true child of the author's feelings and his lived experience.

As far as my literary career is concerned I never felt that it exists in parts or as a patchwork of bits and pieces. It is, in fact, an integral whole with a biological continuity and completeness. My views on metaphysical and physical subjects of human concern are not disjointed or are soldering of two dissimilar theories together forcefully or artificially. My literature genuinely represents my life. It reflects my views and experiences truthfully. My *In Defence of People & Poetry* and for that matter, even my essay on *Savitri* (ref: *Bharati*) do indicate this position clearly.

I do not look upon human being as a complete harmonious entity. He is in fact a hotchpotch of many thoughts, ideas, and feelings. This is what the external world does to him. He is after all the sculptured product of life, is therefore necessarily a conglomeration of contradictions and internal battles. This is the truthful picture of man that a correct cognition of him offers to us. Writers are not sages but only truthful men. And mankind does benefit by truth. Please do not misunderstand I am defending myself. In fact, as you and I know, all defences are again other points of view only. Before I close I am tempted to quote Albert Camus:

> it is better in my opinion to give the era its due since it demands this so vigorously and calmly admit that the period of the revered master, of the artist with a camellia in his button hplf, pf the arm-chair genius is over. To create today is to create dangerously. Any publication is an act and that act exposes one to the passions of the age that forgives nothing. The question for all those who can't live without art and what it signifies, is merely to find out how among the police forces of so many ideologies the strange liberty of creation is possible.

We return to Hyderabad on the 19th September. It is always refreshing to get your letters; they land my mind in new pastures of thought and invigorate new adventures.

With affectionate regards,

Yours sincerely,
Seshendra Sarma

* * * * *

Bombay
September 18, 1989

My Dear Dr. Ramakrishna,

Looking through my papers after returning from Greece I came across a questionnaire you had sent me and the answers I had written. I was thinking of sending those to you. Do indicate when you will be free. Are you likely to be in Hyderabad in October?

I have no influence over Seshendra's writings. He is very obstinate with his freedom; his world of thought and action cannot be altered by anybody. I realised that even before getting married to him. He expresses himself as he wishes. I have come to believe that a writer is "Swayambhoo."

Dr. Mulk Raj Anand came to see us before we left for Greece. He was again reminding me that my autobiography is overdue and that he would get me a publisher. He said, "your story is more important than Gayatri Devi or Vijaya Raje Scindhia. You have lived another kind of life and seen literature at close quarters." Those words were very encouraging. I shall pick up the thread again soon.

With kind regards to you both.

Yours sincerely,
Indira Devi Dhanrajgir

* * * * *

Hyderabad
March 30, 1990

Dear Ramakrishna,

I was extremely happy to receive your letter dated 7.03.1990. It is only the appreciation of the enlightened and learned people like you that matters to me.

My most hearty Ugadi Greetings to you and your family.

Yours always,
Seshendra Sarma

* * * * *

Hyderabad
July 8, 1990

My Dear Dr. Ramakrishna,

I have not heard from you for a long time. But you are in our thoughts. Today we received the Preface of *Nikiforus Vrattakos* translated into English and some of the excerpts were typed out for the press interview. You perhaps don't know that the Greek translation is out and very beautifully produced. Pity I have only a single copy with me, but I have asked for more.

Look forward to hearing from you.

With our regards to you both.

Yours sincerely,
Seshendra Sarma

* * * * *

Warangal
July 11, 1990

Dear Sri Seshendra Sarma,

Thank you for your letter of July 8. I've been under the impression that both of you had gone to Ooty and other places. I'm delighted to know that the Greek translation of *My Country, My People* is out. Mr. Vrattakos's Preface is warm and insightful, stated in good English. By the way, when is your corrected English version going to be published? I'm afraid some of the translations including Vrattakos's were done before corrections. The corrected and revised version comes closer to your original Telugu.

I will see you when I go to Hyderabad next time. For the whole of June I was at my place Eluru, just relaxing. I'm busy completing the MSS of two of my books on Poe.

Regards,

Sincerely,
D. Ramakrishna

* * * * *

Hyderabad
July 11, 1997

Dear Dr. Ramakrishna,

We returned from Ooty last month on 9th June. Coming here we entered the heat wave. It still continues. Only rains will give respite. But are the rains coming or have they missed their way?

The Deccan Chronicle brought out a Special Supplement on Hyderabad to celebrate their 60 years. Before we left for Ooty, they had asked me to contribute an article. So I wrote on Nizam VII. In case you have not seen it, I am enclosing a xerox.

We are well; hope you both are the same. We shall be here for the next 3 months for sure. In November Seshendra has to deliver an extension lecture entitled "Ashram Kayva Yuga—Valmiki to Kalidas." He has not begun writing it yet.

With our fond regards to both of you,

Yours sincerely,
Indira Devi Dhanrajgir

* * * * *

Warangal
July 15, 1997

Dear Sri Seshendra & Smt. Indira Devi,

Thank you for the letter of July 11 and the enclosures. I've quite enjoyed reading your writings in the newspapers, particularly the pieces on Nizam VII and Salman Rushdie. Both are admirable, one for the praise and the other for the condemnation. In his "Open Letter to Salman Rushdie," the Bengali writer rightly dismissed Rushdie as a fool and an ignoramus (*Indian Express*, 13.07.1997). Seshendra too has done well in his piece in Telugu. It's a pity the editors of *The New Yorker* took Rushdie as an authority on Indian life and literature! The widespread condemnation of the man for such writing is more than a "fatwa." It's his literary and cultural hanging from India. And he deserves exposure for parading his ignorance, of course, in articulate English.

With warm regards,

Yours sincerely,
D. Ramakrishna

* * * * *

Hyderabad
July 17, 1997

Dear Dr. Ramakrishna,

We were both happy to get your letter yesterday. You agree with Seshendra's condemnation; it made him feel good. And I thank you for going through my article on the Nizam. Now foreign publishers are contacting me to write about the inside-world of that family. Incidentally, I am the only person left who has known them at close quarters. Seshendra has different views. He says I should not. I am torn between the two. This kind of writing is easy, because I have lived it.

Do you know I never intended to write about Hyderabad? I am positive there is something beyond myself which is getting me write it. Do you believe in such things?

If you decided to come on the 22/23rd, we shall put you up at the Brindavan Hotel and on the 24th you could shift to the University. I would have put you up in the guestroom but right now it is dumped with suitcases and other things. It is not livable. So please telephone me when you get this letter and we can come to a decision. We do want to see you. You may bring your wife also.

In haste to catch the morning post.

With affectionate regards from us to you both.

Yours sincerely,
Indira Devi Dhanrajgir